BAD GIRLS of FASHION

STYLE REBELS FROM CLEOPATRA TO LADY GAGA

JENNIFER CROLL

illustrated by ADA BUCHHOLC

annick press
toronto + berkeley

For my mother, Judy, and my Nana Margaret and Nana Lynn, the original bad girls in my life—J.C.

We acknowledge the support of the Canada Council
for the Arts, the Ontario Arts Council, and the
Government of Canada for our publishing activities.

ONTARIO ARTS COUNCIL
CONSEIL DES ARTS DE L'ONTARIO
an Ontario government agency
un organisme du gouvernement de l'Ontario

Funded by the   Financé par le
Government   gouvernement   Canada
of Canada   du Canada

Distributed in Canada by University of Toronto Press.
Distributed in the U.S.A. by Publishers Group West.
Printed in China

Visit us at: www.annickpress.com
Visit Jennifer Croll at: www.jencroll.com
Visit Ada Buchholc at: www.adabuchholc.pl

Also available in e-book format. Please visit
www.annickpress.com/ebooks.html for
more details.

Cataloging in Publication

Croll, Jennifer, author
Bad girls of fashion : style rebels from
Cleopatra to Lady Gaga / Jennifer Croll ;
illustrated by Ada Buchholc.

Includes bibliographical references and index.
Issued in print and electronic formats.
ISBN 978-1-55451-785-5 (paperback).
ISBN 978-1-55451-786-2 (hardback).
ISBN 978-1-55451-787-9 (html).
ISBN 978-1-55451-788-6 (pdf)

1. Fashion—History—Juvenile literature.
2. Women's clothing—History—Juvenile literature.
3. Celebrities—Clothing—Juvenile literature.
4. Costume—History—Juvenile literature.
5. Women—Biography—Juvenile literature.
6. Celebrities—Biography—Juvenile literature.
I. Buchholc, Ada, illustrator
II. Title.

GT1720.C76 2016   j391'.20922   C2016-900597-6

Contents

Introduction

When you get out of bed in the morning, open your closet, and pick out clothes for the day, what's going through your mind? Maybe you're thinking about how what you wear will help you fit in with the cool crowd, or how a photo of your perfectly color-coordinated ensemble will get a lot of "likes" online. Maybe there's someone you want to impress, or to imitate. Or maybe your deepest thought about your wardrobe is "Do I have a clean shirt today?"

But dressing doesn't always have to be about convenience or fitting in. A pair of heavy boots and a punk T-shirt could make other students think you're tough; an ultra-fashionable dress might cause them to assume you're sophisticated; a flamboyant, brightly colored getup could make them imagine you're creative or free-spirited. Clothes can sometimes have consequences: the "wrong" look could get you kicked out of school, passed over for a job, or branded with a reputation you don't want. But your clothes can also help you get your way or change people's minds about who you are.

Throughout history, people—especially women—have used fashion to shape the way other people think about them. That's partly because it was one of the only ways they could. In the past, women often faced very severe limitations on the careers they could pursue and the kind of life they could live: sometimes dressing up was the only way they could really express themselves. But some women realized how tactical fashion can be—how powerful a tool it is for shaping opinion and for challenging the status quo. And while a lot of other things have changed—women in many countries today have the freedom to choose their own careers and live their lives the way they decide to—fashion still has the power to transform.

This book is all about the bad girls throughout history who have dressed to shake things up. Whether they used clothing to gain power, rebel against social norms, or explore their own identity, the forty-three women in this book—queens, actresses, fashion designers, writers, artists, dancers, politicians, academics, socialites, models, musicians, and activists—used fashion to help them change opinions, confront opposition, and make other people look at them in a different light. Across different eras and social settings, they were willing to take risks in order to get what they wanted; they dressed in ways that weren't socially acceptable, that could have cost them their careers, relationships, or reputations. Sometimes, they didn't just change their own lives: they changed the world around them. And as you read about the daring (and sometimes dangerous) clothing worn by women as diverse as the powerful ancient Egyptian queen Cleopatra, the cross-dressing movie star Marlene Dietrich, and the ultra-arty contemporary pop star Lady Gaga, you'll realize that fashion is anything but frivolous.

ORNATE DRESS

HAT

FAN

PAGE 12

PAGE 81

PAGE 101

PAGE 188

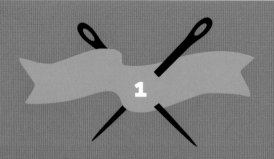

Cleopatra

FASHION

Leader

FULL NAME:
Cleopatra VII Philopator

BORN:
69 BCE, Alexandria, Egypt

OCCUPATION:
Pharaoh of Egypt

BAD GIRL CRED:
Cleopatra knew image was power—
and over two thousand years later,
her image still holds our fascination.

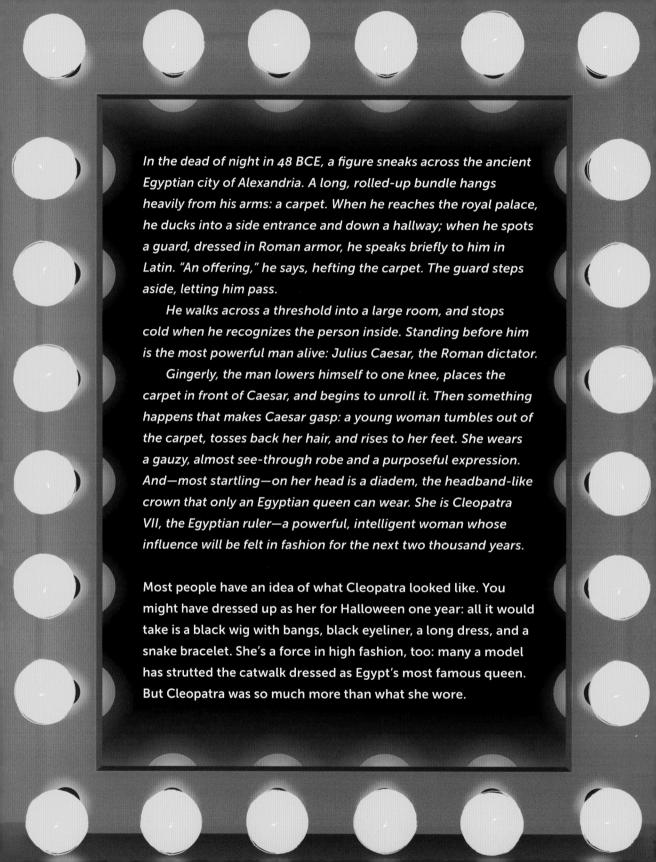

In the dead of night in 48 BCE, a figure sneaks across the ancient Egyptian city of Alexandria. A long, rolled-up bundle hangs heavily from his arms: a carpet. When he reaches the royal palace, he ducks into a side entrance and down a hallway; when he spots a guard, dressed in Roman armor, he speaks briefly to him in Latin. "An offering," he says, hefting the carpet. The guard steps aside, letting him pass.

He walks across a threshold into a large room, and stops cold when he recognizes the person inside. Standing before him is the most powerful man alive: Julius Caesar, the Roman dictator.

Gingerly, the man lowers himself to one knee, places the carpet in front of Caesar, and begins to unroll it. Then something happens that makes Caesar gasp: a young woman tumbles out of the carpet, tosses back her hair, and rises to her feet. She wears a gauzy, almost see-through robe and a purposeful expression. And—most startling—on her head is a diadem, the headband-like crown that only an Egyptian queen can wear. She is Cleopatra VII, the Egyptian ruler—a powerful, intelligent woman whose influence will be felt in fashion for the next two thousand years.

Most people have an idea of what Cleopatra looked like. You might have dressed up as her for Halloween one year: all it would take is a black wig with bangs, black eyeliner, a long dress, and a snake bracelet. She's a force in high fashion, too: many a model has strutted the catwalk dressed as Egypt's most famous queen. But Cleopatra was so much more than what she wore.

WALK LIKE AN
Egyptian

Almost from birth, Cleopatra knew her image was powerful. She grew up in the Egyptian capital of Alexandria, one of five children of the pharaoh Ptolemy XII Auletes. Since Egyptian people associated their royal family with gods, they called young Cleopatra *Thea*, meaning "goddess." She took the message to heart.

Growing up, Cleopatra was never a great beauty, but it didn't matter: she got everywhere with her brains and personality. She threw herself wholeheartedly into learning. Her father was a sponsor of both the Museum of Alexandria and the famous Library of Alexandria, so Cleopatra took advantage of their resources.

She immersed herself in philosophy and history and wrote books on medicine, her favorite topic. She learned nine languages, including Egyptian: she was the first in her family to learn the local tongue.

Cleopatra's family was actually from Macedonia, a small country beside Greece that built a huge empire under the king Alexander the Great.

EGYPT AND ROME

During Cleopatra's time, Egypt was a "client kingdom" of Rome, which meant that Egyptian rulers had to report to Roman leadership. Egypt operated independently, but only with the permission of Roman rulers, who could snatch that independence away at any moment.

Her ancestor Ptolemy I was one of Alexander the Great's generals, and when Alexander died and his empire was broken into pieces, Ptolemy was given Egypt. His family had ruled it ever since.

By age sixteen, Cleopatra was pharaoh. At first, she co-ruled with her father. Her family was complicated, to say the least: the Ptolemies didn't mind incest in the slightest, and married each other to keep power within the family. In fact, Cleopatra's father's only official wife, who had died years earlier, was both his cousin and his niece (nobody knows for sure who Cleopatra's mother was). Rising to the throne, Cleopatra was given the title *Thea Philopator:* "father-loving goddess." When her father died less than a year later, in March, the quick-witted teenager knew she couldn't take her power for granted. She'd inevitably be married to one of her brothers, as was the family tradition—and she didn't intend to share command. So she continued to sign documents in her father's name and pretended nothing had changed. After four months of planning, on the thirtieth of June, 51 BCE, she let the Senate know about her father's death—and then launched a grand tour of Egyptian temples to get the rural population on her side.

When she dressed every day, Cleopatra mixed Greek (or Macedonian) and Roman styles to please her subjects while paying homage to her roots. After all, she was a Macedonian woman who ruled over a country that was, technically, part of the Roman empire. She wore belted tunics and mantles (a type of cloak) that fell to the ankle in vibrant shades of blue, green, and red, with woven sandals on her feet. But on *this* trip, Cleopatra dressed more tactically. She wore a red and white crown to symbolize a united Egypt (white represented Upper Egypt; red, Lower Egypt). Cleopatra also knew how important gods were to the Egyptian people, and realized she would have an easier time leading if people saw her as a kind of goddess. So she styled herself as the *Nea* ("new") *Isis*.

As Nea Isis, Cleopatra wore a white linen sheath decorated with sequins and beads, and draped over it a black robe with a tasseled fringe. On her head, she wore a crown with ram and cow horns, a sun disc, and feathers of Isis. She threw on a wig for public appearances, and the rest of the time pulled her hair back in a braided bun that has been dubbed her "melon hairstyle." Snake bracelets were another carefully planned touch, since the goddess Isis was often portrayed with

Cleopatra as Nea Isis.
Previous page: An important deity within Egyptian mythology, Isis was the goddess of motherhood, nature, and magic.

a snake. As Isis's lookalike, Cleopatra spoke to her subjects—many of whom were illiterate—visually: she was a divine leader, and worthy of their devotion. One look at her, and they knew more than a thousand written decrees could tell them.

Girl BOSS

Julius Caesar: Cleopatra's key to securing power.

Though her subjects loved her, Cleopatra found herself in a dangerous position in 50 BCE, when her much younger brother Ptolemy XIII was named her coruler. Egged on by his advisers, who weren't fans of Cleopatra, he pushed her out of Alexandria—and so she waited, out in the desert, with troops loyal to her leadership. That's where she was the fateful moment that Julius Caesar, the Roman leader, arrived in Alexandria to collect on a loan to her family and raise money for his next military campaign.

Just how Cleopatra wound up in Caesar's private chambers is something historians argue about. The most popular story (and the one that's usually portrayed in movies) involves her rolling out of a carpet, but other interpretations depict her being carried inside a sack, or simply walking through the city cloaked in a face-shrouding himation.

Whether she was carried or walked there herself, Cleopatra's appearance before Caesar was a daring feat. In that moment, she was dressed to impress: both queenly and seductive. Though he was already married, Caesar was well known for his love affairs with women, a fact Cleopatra probably knew and planned to exploit. Whether it was that night or in the following days, she became Caesar's lover, sneakily securing his support of her leadership bid—and, most important, of Egypt's continuing independence, as Caesar could easily have decided to bring Egypt under direct Roman leadership. Caesar and Cleopatra's relationship was politically and personally good for both of them, and it brought Cleopatra her first child, a boy she named after his father: Caesarion.

But things couldn't go smoothly forever, and in 44 BCE, the worst thing that could happen *did* happen. Caesar, recently declared dictator for life, was killed by a group led by a Roman senator, Brutus. He was literally stabbed in the back, which is where this expression, which means "betrayed," comes from. In that moment, Cleopatra lost her most powerful supporter, and, with him, her guarantee of the Egyptian throne. But the wily queen wasn't going to let that get in the way of ruling the country she loved.

HIMATION

A cloak made from fabric wrapped around the body. When Cleopatra was alive, Greek-born women wrapped their himatia tightly around themselves in public, concealing their faces from everyone except their husbands.

ICONIC LOOK № 1

ORNATE DRESS

HAT

FAN

UNBOUND FEET

EMPRESS DOWAGER CIXI

EMPRESS DOWAGER CIXI played a huge role in the fashion of young Chinese women in the nineteenth century. Cixi, nicknamed "Dragon Lady" in the West, had a fierce reputation to match. Born a concubine, she eventually seized the throne. One of the ways Cixi gained favor while in power was being photographed in glamorous attire, but her most important move was abolishing footbinding. Footbinding was a very fashionable practice in China—and a painful one, too—in which a young girl's feet were broken and then tied up tightly to prevent them from growing. Cixi's late-in-life ruling gave other women the freedom to walk freely, as she did.

FASHION SPOTLIGHT
Elizabeth I

FULL NAME:

Elizabeth I

BORN:

1533, Greenwich, England

OCCUPATION:

Queen of England

BAD GIRL CRED:

**Refusing to marry, Elizabeth retained power
with a brilliant propaganda campaign we
still remember today.**

If you do a Google search for Elizabeth I, you'll find lots of images that look pretty much the same: a young, pale-skinned, ferociously red-haired queen with a crown on her head and a big, puffy white collar around her neck. It's amazing—even after her death, this powerful queen, one of England's most famous leaders, still controls what we think of her.

"The Virgin Queen": that was Elizabeth I's nickname. Queen at a time when people didn't trust female leadership, from the moment she took the throne Elizabeth was under a lot of pressure to marry and have a baby. Yet, despite interested suitors, she never did. Her supporters suggested that her true marriage was to her country, but Elizabeth herself likely knew that staying single would let her keep a hold on power that would have been diminished with the arrival of a husband or a son. Her good leadership ushered in a golden age, particularly in the arts: Elizabethan England was the era of Shakespeare. But it was her nimble manipulation of appearance that made her subjects love her.

The daughter of Henry VIII and Anne Boleyn (whom Henry infamously beheaded on dubious charges of treason), Elizabeth was crowned in 1559 at age twenty-five. At first she was a cautious ruler, and dressed demurely to show it: her look involved cone-shaped skirts and puffed sleeves. But as she grew more confident, her clothes became more showy too. She picked ostentatious outfits to impress her subjects, like dresses with plunging, cleavage-revealing necklines, huge hoop skirts, lace ruffs, and lots of fans with jeweled handles. And impress they did: aristocratic ladies began dressing like her, and Elizabeth intentionally ignored the laws that would have punished anyone who attempted to mimic her. Poorer subjects who couldn't afford Elizabeth's fancy clothing did what they could, buying cameos or metal disks stamped with the queen's image. Others dyed their hair bright red in honor of Elizabeth, history's first fashionable redhead.

There's a reason why we still have such a clear image of Elizabeth—and that's the propaganda campaign she waged using fashion and imagery. Despite her popularity, some doubted the abilities of a female ruler, and Elizabeth came up with a way to change their minds with symbolism. Instead of growing old, like a normal woman would, she would present herself as an eternally youthful goddess, playing up the idea that she was still a virgin. (Whether she actually was, no one knows for sure.) To do this, she sat for a small number of portraits from which all further images of her were to be made. These portraits showed a young Elizabeth—so even as the real Elizabeth aged, paintings of her never did. (Historians call this Elizabeth's "Mask of Youth.")

Elizabeth I's portraits were also loaded with symbols that spoke to her subjects in a kind of code. Moons and pearls tied Elizabeth to Diana, the virgin goddess of Roman mythology. Elizabeth was often pictured with an ermine (a kind of weasel), whose white coat symbolized purity. Also making frequent appearances was the white Tudor rose: while it honored the royal Tudor family, it was also a medieval symbol for the Virgin Mary, mother of Jesus. All these hidden messages shaped perceptions of the queen and helped form what people call the "cult of Elizabeth." The queen's subjects didn't just serve her; they also worshipped her, in the same way they might have done with a goddess, as Cleopatra's subjects did.

By the time Elizabeth I died, she owned more than two thousand awe-inspiring items of clothing. She was sixty-nine years old—but even today, when people think of her, they picture the young, flame-haired queen in all her portraits. The Mask of Youth has preserved Elizabeth forever.

The Darnley portrait, painted around 1575, was the model for many later portraits of Elizabeth.

SAVING HER KINGDOM, *Again*

In 41 BCE, crowds gather along the river Kypros outside the city of Tarsus, anxious to catch a glimpse of the spectacle everyone is gossiping about. There, gliding down the river, is a sight unlike anything they've seen in their lives: a glorious, golden barge, with royal purple sails flying majestically. The figure reclining below the sails, they know, is a goddess: she wears a gauzy chiton— a Greek-style robe—with one shoulder provocatively revealed and opulent strands of expensive pearls around her slender neck. Her hair is in ringlets and her eyes are heavily rimmed with black kohl. Boys languidly fan her. "Aphrodite!" gasps one of the onlookers.

Opposite: Cleopatra receiving Mark Antony.

After Caesar's death, Rome needed a new ruler. This big job was taken over by a three-man council (a "triumvirate"): Mark Antony, Caesar's adopted son Octavian, and Marcus Aemilius Lepidus. The three men split the Roman territories, and Antony ended up with Egypt. But there were power struggles among the three, and Antony was concerned with his image. To make himself look powerful, Antony declared himself a modern-day Dionysus, the revered god of wine and debauchery. He summoned Cleopatra to Tarsus (a city in today's Turkey) so that he could figure out where her loyalties lay and whether he could still trust her with Egypt. And Cleopatra, not one to be outdone, came up with a plot to subdue Dionysus: she dressed up as Aphrodite, the Greek goddess of love.

When Antony boarded Cleopatra's golden barge, the romantic suggestion that the pharaoh had set up with her clever styling couldn't have been more clear, and Antony couldn't help himself.

When Antony and Cleopatra were married in 37 BCE, coins were issued that portrayed Cleopatra with melon hairdo and diadem. But a closer look reveals that the Macedonian pharaoh's portrait looks more than a little Roman. In the ancient world, coins were a powerful way of crafting a ruler's image, and historians think Cleopatra was visually mixing dynasties to cement her power.

Drama followed Cleopatra to her death. As time went on, the rivalry within the triumvirate ruling Rome escalated into war, and finally, Octavian's forces attacked Antony's at Alexandria. When it looked like Octavian was winning, Antony's armies deserted him to join the victor, and Cleopatra, thinking Antony must have perished, told her servants to tell anyone asking that she was dead. Hearing this false news, Antony stabbed himself in the stomach. Cleopatra—of course still very much alive—summoned her wounded lover, who was brought to her. He died in her arms.

Things looked very dire for Cleopatra, and she was terrified that Octavian would humiliate her and march her through the streets in chains. In her mind, death was a better option than being scorned by her subjects. So she dug deep into the medical knowledge she'd gained during her childhood years in the Library of

Cleopatra's dramatic death inspired a lot of art, including this statue.

Alexandria. Thinking of all the ways to bring death painlessly and easily, she came to a daring conclusion: the best answer was the bite of a cobra. The details of this very famous ending to Cleopatra's life are uncertain—some say a live cobra bit her on the arm, but others think smart Cleopatra had kept a vial of the poison stored away, just in case. Either way, she perished from snake venom at the age of thirty-nine.

CELEBRITIES WHO HAVE DRESSED AS CLEOPATRA

KATY PERRY

"Dark Horse" video, 2014

BLAKE LIVELY

on *The Martha Stewart Show*, 2008

BRITNEY SPEARS

Elizabeth Arden advertisement, 2012

KIM KARDASHIAN

Harper's Bazaar fashion magazine, 2011

HEIDI KLUM

Halloween, 2012

CLEOPATRA, the Star!

It's easy to imagine Cleopatra as a stylish, powerful queen, but since she was alive almost two thousand years ago, it's tough to say where myth and reality meet. Her image was greatly shaped by histories written by spiteful Romans, who hated her for her influence over both Caesar and Mark Antony. They portrayed her as a wanton woman, a glamorous and immoral seductress, though in modern times, many people view her as a brilliant political strategist. Given the great drama of her life, she has often been the subject of fiction and art, beginning with Shakespeare's famous play *Antony and Cleopatra,* which added some untrue flourishes for the sake of drama (for example, Shakespeare has the cobra bite her on the breast).

Cleopatra's big-screen debut was in the earliest years of film—an 1899 short horror film about the resurrection of her mummy. More famous is a silent film from 1917 starring one of the most popular stars of the time, Theda Bara.

To portray Cleopatra's wealth, the production spent shocking quantities of money, and Bara wore sexy costumes that later led to the film being branded obscene. The 1934 version starring Claudette Colbert was similarly over-the-top, and inspired department stores like Macy's to sell Cleopatra-inspired gowns and shoes.

Aside from ancient Roman rumor-mongers, easily the biggest influence on Cleopatra's modern image was the 1963 film starring one of the twentieth century's biggest stars, Elizabeth Taylor. *Cleopatra* was an expensive epic that made headlines with its scandals: Taylor had an affair with her married costar, Richard Burton, who played Mark Antony. But even bigger than the drama was Taylor's larger-than-life public image, which tethered Cleopatra to the film star's vampy silver-screen glamour and forever infused Taylor with Cleopatra's sensual mythology.

Clockwise from bottom left: Elizabeth Taylor; Lillie Langtry in an 1891 stage play; Theda Bara; and a poster for director Cecil B. DeMille's 1934 film.

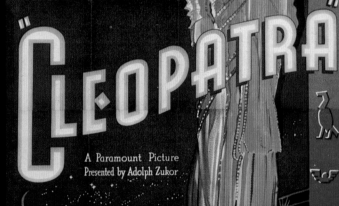

CECIL B. DeMILLE'S

"CLEOPATRA"

A Paramount Picture
Presented by Adolph Zukor

CLAUDETTE COLBERT
WARREN WILLIAM
HENRY WILCOXON
JOSEPH SCHILDKRAUT

COSTLY COSTUMES

Elizabeth Taylor's costumes in *Cleopatra* were the work of Renie Conley, who was so well-known as a costume designer that she went by just her first name. The budget for Taylor's costumes was $194,000—in today's U.S. dollars, that would be $1.5 million. Renie spent the money well, and won an Oscar for her designs.

In the film, Taylor undergoes sixty-five costume changes, all sumptuous robes and tight dresses that emphasize her sexuality rather than historical accuracy. She is adorned with piles of jewelry; her eyes are heavily painted, and she's usually shown with her hair in a bob with bangs. You might think of it as a "Cleopatra cut," but the real Cleopatra, of course, wore a melon-style braided bun. Taylor's hairstyle as Cleopatra was simply one that was popular in the early '60s, and the image stuck. We can also credit the film for the 1960s popularity of arm cuffs, snake jewelry, snake rings, and heavy eye makeup—a commercial for Revlon at the time offered a Cleopatra-inspired product called Sphinx Eyes. And since that decade, Cleopatra has continued to lend her name and image to fashion lines, music videos, books, and films.

It's amazing that for over two thousand years Cleopatra has held such a place in people's imaginations. The Cleopatra we conjure in our minds is as much a product of popular culture and years of stylish imitators as she is a real reflection of one of the first women to realize the power of style. And yet it's impossible to deny her influence: a goddess she wasn't, but Cleopatra's image is truly immortal.

FASHION SPOTLIGHT
Angela Davis

FULL NAME:
Angela Yvonne Davis

BORN:
January 26, 1944, Birmingham, Alabama

OCCUPATION:
Political activist, scholar, author

BAD GIRL CRED:
Iconic for her natural hair, Davis has devoted her life to black equality.

Angela Davis has lived to see her own image turned into an icon of black political resistance. The silhouette of her younger self from the late 1960s, complete with a large Afro, adorns T-shirts and tote bags, buttons and mugs. Young women wear these accessories, or even style themselves after Davis, with a specific intent: to channel her power and align themselves with her politics. Much like another political revolutionary, Che Guevara (a Marxist who played a big role in the Cuban Revolution), her image and style have become a symbol of something much larger than herself.

Born in Alabama, Davis excelled in school and won a scholarship to Brandeis University in Massachusetts, where she was one of only three black students in her year. She went on to graduate studies in Germany, majoring in philosophy. Davis had grown up in an activist family and learned about communist and socialist ideas from an early age, and in Germany she became involved with left-wing student groups. Davis returned in the late 1960s, when she heard about the political situation around black civil rights unfolding in the U.S., including the formation of the Black Panthers. The Black Panthers were a revolutionary organization that campaigned for an end to police brutality and for equal rights for African-Americans. Their philosophy was captured by their slogan: "Black Power." As part of their image, the Panthers adopted a uniform: blue shirts, black pants, black leather jackets, and, most important, black berets.

In 1969 and 1970, Davis taught philosophy and feminism at the University of California in Los Angeles. Her classes were extremely popular, and she was known for her political activism as both a member of the Communist Party and an associate of the Black Panthers. The university tried to fire her for her Communist ties, eventually managing to find a reason for her termination in the inflammatory language she used in speeches (for example, she used the derogatory term "pigs" to refer to police officers). What really landed Davis in the public eye, however, was her association with a black teenager who had kidnapped and killed a judge for political reasons. Though Davis had nothing to do with the crime, she had purchased the weapons that were used, and she was arrested. At her trial, a jury declared her not guilty. It was during the course of this highly publicized event that the nation was exposed to Davis's image: a stylish young woman whose mode of dress combined '70s chic with Black Panther radicalism. She was photographed wearing denim jackets, miniskirts, tinted glasses, and turtlenecks. But it was her hairstyle—a large, natural Afro—that made her an instant icon.

Negative attitudes toward the natural texture of black hair go back centuries. Whites looked down on black people for their physical qualities, like dark skin and coarse, curly hair, using these so-called inferiorities to justify oppression. In the 1960s, respectable black women were expected to straighten their hair with chemicals or hot irons, and even today, most black female celebrities wear their hair straight. So in this environment, Davis's Afro was not just a hairstyle but a radical statement, symbolizing resistance and black pride.

After her moment in the national spotlight, Davis's political career continued, and she has remained a vocal critic of the American prison system and a staunch black feminist. She has struggled with her role as a style icon: she doesn't want the complex politics of the black civil rights movement to be simplified into a shallow fashion statement. But combined with an understanding of black history, her image remains a powerful inspiration to young women passionate about the fight for equality.

Davis rocking her natural Afro in Moscow's Red Square in 1972.

Marie Antoinette

FASHION

Decadent

FULL NAME:
Maria Antonia Josepha Johanna

BORN:
November 2, 1755, Vienna, Austria

OCCUPATION:
Queen of France

BAD GIRL CRED:
Did her clothing really provoke a revolution?
Maybe not, but no woman in history was as
hated for her fashion as Marie Antoinette.

On a summer's day in a park in the middle of Paris, a group of pretty young women recline lazily on the grass, eating ripe strawberries and cream from delicate white bowls and chattering happily. They wear gauzy dresses with layers of skirts, which spread out around them, but the most startling thing about them is their hair. It's very tall, stark white, and decorated with ornaments. The woman with the tallest hair is the clear center of attention. She leans back, cooling herself with a tiny fan, and observes the park around her. Everyone is watching her; people have gathered along the walkways in small groups, looking in her direction. But it also seems that many of these people have seen her before: throughout the crowd, there are women who are dressed just like her. Elaborate dresses. Tall white hair dotted with ornaments. Little fans. Noticing this, the woman— Marie Antoinette, the last queen of France—smiles. She has always wanted to influence her subjects, and seeing the way they imitate her, she knows she has.

You might know her as the queen with the big, poofy white hair, the one who said "Let them eat cake!" Even today, Marie Antoinette is remembered for flaunting her expensive taste and for making ostentatious—and, some would say, disrespectful— fashion choices. But she wasn't just dressing up for the fun of it: Marie Antoinette's fashion choices were all about seizing power over her kingdom, the sort of power she couldn't get any other way.

A CONVENIENT
Arrangement

Marie Antoinette was groomed for the throne from a very young age. Her parents were the emperor and empress of Austria; from birth she was an archduchess. She grew up at court, and was educated mostly in things like music, dance, appearance, and manners. When she was a little girl,

she also enjoyed playing with dolls and dressing them up; she took to wearing fancy dresses herself to match.

The negotiation for Marie Antoinette's marriage was finalized when she was only thirteen years old. Within royal families, marriages were almost always arranged. They were political bonds, not romantic

physical appearance. They thought she wasn't attractive enough, and they specifically demanded, as part of the negotiations, that she fix her crooked teeth, get a more flattering hairdo, and assemble a more "fashionable" (to the French, that meant "French") wardrobe. Marie Antoinette had no choice in the matter: her family spared no expense giving her a dramatic makeover. A painting was commissioned of the newly coiffed archduchess and sent to the French court. Upon seeing it, the deal was done. Maria Antonia had to take a new French name, too: Marie Antoine. Only later, in France, did she become known as Marie Antoinette (a diminutive nickname).

The following year, when she was fourteen, Marie Antoinette began her long journey from Austria to Versailles, just outside Paris, in a horse-drawn glass carriage called a *berline*. She had her first rude awakening about the realities of court life as soon as she hit the border of Austria and France, when she was handed over to representatives

ones, usually set up to begin, strengthen, or reinforce diplomatic relationships between countries. And so, when Marie Antoinette's mother began to negotiate her potential marriage to the French dauphin (prince) Louis-Auguste, the young girl was discussed like she was a piece of property to be traded. The biggest issue holding up the deal, from the French side, was Marie Antoinette's

The palace of Versailles was home to French royalty beginning in the 1600s.

from the French court. There, right at the border, the ladies took her into a pavilion, where they stripped her of all her expensive clothing while she cried and the rest of the entourage watched. They then dressed her in a new ensemble: a low-cut golden gown with panniers (hoops meant to accentuate the hips) and whalebone stays (to make her waist look slender). They dusted her hair with white powder and added heavy rouge to her tear-streaked cheeks, and the transformation was complete. Marie Antoinette was now French.

TOILETTE

The *toilette* was a daily dressing ritual for French royals. Members of the court and other hangers-on would enter the chambers of the royal in question to observe him or her being groomed and putting on clothing. For Marie Antoinette, this involved extended periods of nudity and semi-undress in front of strangers, which was quite a shock to the young princess.

ROYAL, *Limited*

Snorting and huffing, a boar races through the woods, running for its life. Behind it, dogs howl, tracing its scent, and behind them, horses gallop at full tilt, hooves kicking up the undergrowth. Men ride the horses, all of them in smart, tailored riding gear. But there's one who stands out, riding at the back: a figure smaller than the rest. Strawberry blonde curls peek out from beneath a feathered cap; below that, the rider wears a fitted riding jacket, a ruffled men's collar visible at the top. It takes a second glance to realize: this is a woman. She sits astride her horse like a man, her legs clad in tight, formfitting riding pants (or "breeches"), and rides her horse at a full canter. She's Marie Antoinette, out for the hunt in the woods around Versailles.

Right: Marie Antoinette in 1775, the year she became Queen of France.

Soon after she arrived at Versailles in 1770, Marie Antoinette was wed to the dauphin, Louis, who was fifteen years old. On her wedding day, she wore a dazzling silver dress with full skirts and panniers, accessorized with many diamonds—she truly sparkled. After the ceremony and the feasting, though, Marie Antoinette faced a real challenge: consummation. It was a long-standing tradition for French royals to consummate their union in front of a crowd of nobles, religious figures, and relatives. This would prove the new couple was going to work on producing a baby boy who would be heir to the throne. After a ceremony in which an archbishop blessed their bed with holy water, the two lay down and the curtains of the four-poster were shut behind them. But then, to Marie Antoinette's horror, Louis-Auguste simply rolled over and fell asleep. There was no consummation.

A French queen, which Marie Antoinette would be one day, did not actually have a lot of power. Her primary role was to produce an heir to the throne; if she couldn't do that, she was failing at her job. Marie Antoinette wasn't off to a good start. Despite her constant flirting with and cajoling of Louis, their relationship remained unconsummated into the weeks ahead. Instead of spending time with his winsome new wife, Louis-Auguste preferred riding and other hobbies—all of which caused people at court to gossip. So, too, did the court gossip when Marie Antoinette, who hated the restrictive new clothing that the French court required, abandoned wearing her uncomfortable whalebone corset.

SEIZING
the Reins

Marie Antoinette dressed for the hunt in 1771.

Looking for a way to fill her time, escape judgment, and find freedom, Marie Antoinette took up riding. The outfit she wore on horseback defied convention: ladies, at the time, wore skirts over their breeches if they wore breeches at all. But Marie Antoinette preferred to dress as the men did. She also liked to follow the hunt, which she'd been advised against. In 1771, when her mother asked that she have her portrait painted, Marie Antoinette posed triumphantly in her riding gear, on the back of a horse. The image evoked an enormously famous portrait of Louis XIV, the so-called Sun King, and Marie Antoinette's mimicry was a provocative visual claim of power.

Marie Antoinette's riding also brought her closer to Louis, and by 1772, they finally consummated their union. For the time being, her power was secured. In 1775, Louis-Auguste ascended the throne, becoming Louis XVI—and Marie Antoinette was queen. For the ceremony, she wore a dress covered in heavy jewels, created by a designer named Rose Bertin and considered very modern at the time. Her hair was piled high, powdered, and decorated with feathers—the first step toward her signature hairstyle, the pouf. Another invention of Bertin, the pouf involved wire, cloth, horsehair, and a liberal dusting of powder. These hair sculptures were sometimes up to three feet tall and were woven with decorations that delivered some sort of message. One of Marie Antoinette's more elaborate poufs, worn to celebrate her husband's smallpox inoculation, bore symbols of Greek medicine, including serpents, an olive tree, and a sun; others featured an assortment of vegetables or a model ship.

Thrilled with her new look, Marie Antoinette made the day trip to Paris several times a week to show off different versions. This was unusual for French queens, who typically stayed within the safety of Versailles. But Marie Antoinette enjoyed the attention, and by promenading around Paris in her daring fashions, she inspired legions of imitators. She even allowed them to visit Rose Bertin's shop—another unusual move, as royals typically required that shopkeepers maintain an exclusive contract with them. Soon, a pouf and a Rose Bertin dress were the necessary uniform for every French lady of a certain rank, and Marie Antoinette had won over France ... for a time.

Unfortunately, some women spent nearly all their money in attempts to dress like the queen. Many said at the time that they'd rather spend their time dressing up their hair in poufs than trying to get married, so Marie Antoinette was seen as a subversive force, degrading the morals of young Frenchwomen. And as women from all social classes began to dress lavishly and provocatively like her, class distinctions fell away, and it was harder to tell a prostitute from an aristocrat. The blame for this perceived impropriety fell squarely on Marie Antoinette.

LOUIS XIV

Louis XIV was an extremely powerful French king and the great-great-grandfather of Marie Antoinette's husband, Louis XVI. He was wise to the power of fashion to shape opinion, and always dressed flamboyantly in rich clothing to reinforce his royal image. He also commissioned hundreds of portraits of himself to make sure nobody forgot how kingly he was at all times.

ICONIC LOOK Nº 2

IMELDA MARCOS

IMELDA MARCOS was the First Lady of the Philippines from 1965 to 1986, but she's probably best known for her shoes. Her husband's rule was infamously corrupt, and to present a powerful image, Marcos led a lavish lifestyle, organizing enormous parties, flying in private jets—and buying expensive clothing. Eventually, there was a revolution in the Philippines. When Marcos and her family fled, her vast stash of gowns, handbags, and shoes was discovered. The world was aghast. Though Marcos eventually returned to the Philippines and continues to work in politics, nobody has ever forgotten her excesses, and her famous shoes—over three thousand pairs!—are part of the collection of the National Museum of the Philippines.

FASHION SPOTLIGHT
Rose Bertin

FULL NAME:
Marie-Jeanne Rose Bertin

BORN:
July 2, 1747, Abbeville, France

OCCUPATION:
Dressmaker, milliner, fashion designer

BAD GIRL CRED:
**In a time when women couldn't run businesses,
Bertin's boutique defined the fashions of an era.**

In the eighteenth century, there weren't many careers for women, and laws banned women from pursuing jobs in most fields. This was true of fashion, too, where women were usually assistants, not entrepreneurs. But that didn't stop Rose Bertin—an ambitious, unmarried young woman—from becoming the leading fashion designer of her time.

The daughter of a nurse, Bertin moved to Paris at age sixteen to apprentice under a milliner (hatmaker) named Mademoiselle Pagalle; Bertin eventually became Pagalle's business partner. In that shop, she successfully made hats for many French aristocrats. In 1770, when she was twenty-four, she openly broke the law that stated that only male mercers (cloth sellers) could operate shops that sold fashionable embellishments for ladies' attire. She opened up her own store, Le Grand Mogol, and operated as a *marchande de modes* (female fashion merchant). She hired a staff of thirty women and filled the store with an elaborate assortment of accessories and full ensembles, many of them unique designs. In 1774, she added to that selection a hairstyle she called the "pouf." Fatefully, that year, one of Bertin's most loyal customers from the aristocracy introduced her to the woman who would become her most important client: Marie Antoinette.

Marie Antoinette instantly fell in love with the pouf, and put Bertin on her payroll. Alongside the pouf, Bertin was responsible for designing the trendsetting outfits that Marie Antoinette used to jointly dazzle and offend the French public. Bertin's designs were incredibly ostentatious, and so large that women wearing them took up more space than a single person should. But they were also so popular that they gained international fame, and Bertin was commissioned to make clothing for fashionable ladies as far away as England and Russia. Acknowledging her success, the French government allowed female *marchandes de modes* to form their own guild, meaning that Bertin's business was no longer an illegal venture. But Bertin, being a close associate of Marie Antoinette, was not above criticism. She and Marie Antoinette had become close friends, and the queen even invited Bertin to attend her daily *toilette*—a right typically only extended to the nobility, not working women like Bertin. The public was suspicious both of Bertin's success as a female entrepreneur and of her closeness to their monarch, and began calling her the Minister of Fashion, suggesting that she held more power than she was due.

And yet, when the French Revolution began, Bertin's business kept going. For a time, she filled the (much smaller) orders Marie Antoinette placed from jail. When she realized that the majority of her upper-class clientele were either being put to death or fleeing the country, Bertin moved her business to London to serve the needs of expat Frenchwomen. Then, in 1795, Bertin moved back to France, which was now a republic, and discovered that tastes had changed: in a country that aspired to equality, her expensive, over-the-top styles didn't fly. She retired in the early 1800s, but her shop had already inspired a big change in fashion, and the rise of the exclusive, custom-fitted clothing known as *couture* owes a big debt to her.

Marie Antoinette wearing Rose Bertin's signature hairstyle, the pouf.

QUEEN AND *Country*

Women frolic in a sun-dappled field, a colonnaded château standing behind them. They sing and they dance, scandalously barefoot, without a care in the world. And they dress like peasants, in loose, white dresses and milkmaid bonnets. But these are no peasants: they're a queen and her mistresses.

Knowing that Marie Antoinette loved getting away from the French court and its rigid ways, in 1774, her husband gave her an important gift: a château called the Petit Trianon. Only a short walk or ride from Versailles, it became Marie Antoinette's very own small kingdom, where she could do whatever she liked. Here, she pursued

from muslin (a light cotton cloth). It was worn with a sash, and sometimes with a bonnet or a simple straw hat. Marie Antoinette began wearing it in 1780; by 1782, it was a popular style in the streets of Paris—but because of its looseness, it was considered tawdry. Even Marie Antoinette's new status as a mother couldn't save her from criticism. (She gave birth to a baby girl in 1778, and to a boy, an heir to the throne, in 1781, then had two more children in the years that followed.) She commissioned a painting of herself in her favorite getup, and it was immediately controversial: some thought the queen had been painted in her underclothes. She was taken to task, too, for popularizing a style from the lower classes, yet again making it difficult to determine a lady's social standing from her attire.

By the time the French Revolution began in 1789, the queen had developed a reputation. Her relentless pursuit of freedom and fashion had made her seem more like a mistress than a wife, so many suspected her of adultery. And her parade of new clothing in Paris and in portraits was seen as immensely wasteful—an unforgivable sin in a country where many were stricken by poverty. (So reviled was she that some accuse her of being one of the

a sort of country life of riding, sports, and fun. Where once she had flaunted her difference by taking opulence to extremes, now she abandoned the rich, gaudy fabrics and styles that dominated clothing at court. Her most daring fashion was the *gaulle*, a white, loose-fitting peasant-style gown made

"LET THEM EAT CAKE!"

is a quote often attributed to Marie Antoinette, but the truth is, she never said it. It actually comes from the autobiography of the philosopher Jean-Jacques Rousseau—written while Marie Antoinette was still a girl—who described the response of "a great princess" after she was told the peasants had no bread. When many people in France were starving, and Marie Antoinette was cavorting in Versailles in fashions they couldn't afford, it was easy to see her as the sort of unsympathetic person who would say something like that. In later accounts of her life, those words became a catchphrase for her cruelty.

causes of the Revolution.) In 1789, she and her family were removed from Versailles and placed in confinement in Paris. They made one failed attempt to escape, but they were soon back in captivity. In 1792, France was declared a republic and the monarchy abolished, and at that moment, Marie Antoinette's fate was sealed. In 1793, she was convicted of treason, and she was put to death by guillotine that same year. On the day she died, at age thirty-seven, Marie Antoinette wore a spotless white dress that one of her mistresses had smuggled to her—her last fashion statement.

Despite her fall from grace, people today are still fascinated by the way Marie Antoinette used daring, over-the-top fashion to seize a powerful role for herself within French society. She was a muse to the filmmaker Sofia Coppola, who in 2006 filmed a whimsical version of Marie Antoinette's life story that very much played up her role as a smart but misunderstood girl stifled by the monarchy. She's been the inspiration for fashion collections, too, by designers like John Galliano, Alexander McQueen, and Christian Lacroix. Almost three hundred years after the Revolution, Marie Antoinette's reign over fashion continues.

FASHION SPOTLIGHT
Wallis Simpson

FULL NAME:

Bessie Wallis Warfield

BORN:

June 19, 1896, Blue Ridge Summit, Pennsylvania

OCCUPATION:

Socialite

BAD GIRL CRED:

**Ultra-fashionable Simpson did whatever she wanted—
like scandalize Britons by running away with their king.**

"That woman"—that's what the British aristocracy snidely called Wallis Simpson, a twice-divorced, middle-aged American socialite who, scandalously, married the man who had been their king. But for Simpson, who was notoriously witty and didn't care about playing by the rules, being *that woman* was just fine.

When Simpson (then Warfield) was very young, her father passed away, leaving her and her mother dependent upon relatives. After attending a fancy boarding school in Maryland on her uncle's dime and then appearing as a Baltimore debutante (she took the bus to have a dress made for the occasion, from her own design, by a local couturier), the young woman thought she had found a good husband in Earl Winfield Spencer, a U.S. Navy pilot. Unfortunately, he turned out to be an alcoholic who liked to lock her in the bathroom. Her second marriage was better: to Ernest Aldrich Simpson, a shipping executive. The two set up home in London, and in 1931, Simpson was introduced to Edward, Prince of Wales and heir to the British throne.

Simpson, by her own admission, was not very pretty. "I'm not a beautiful woman ... so the only thing I can do is dress better than anyone else," she once said. Along with her knack for appearing in impeccable style, she also had undeniable charisma and charm, and that is what drew Edward to her.

By 1934, the prince and Simpson were deep into an affair, and Edward was smitten. He loved Simpson's scathing wit and lack of regard for his royal position. But Edward's love was a huge problem: in 1936, when King George V passed away, Edward became king. It was not accepted for a British monarch to marry someone who had had a divorce—and Simpson was in the process of finalizing a second. But Edward would not be denied: he gave up the throne so he and Simpson could marry, which they did in 1937.

After the marriage, Simpson was demonized by the British press and loathed by the British public. She wasn't just an inappropriate match for Edward: she was a dangerous symbol, too. At a time when it was hard for a woman to get a divorce at all, she'd had two, and then, rather than wallowing in disgrace, she had married not just another man, but a king—one who selfishly abandoned his country for her (becoming Duke of Windsor). She was never accepted by the royal family. But she turned her nose up at them in return; after the new king and queen took the throne, she nicknamed Elizabeth (later known as the Queen Mother) "Cookie," for her appetite, and made fun of her unstylish, frumpy clothes.

Resolute in the face of all this negative press, Simpson was determined to prove she belonged by the side of a former monarch. She used clothing as a defense against criticism, and soon became known as one of the most fashionable women in the world. With money at her disposal, she became an important client of couturiers including Schiaparelli, Dior, Givenchy, and Mainbocher. She was known for wearing sleek, pared-down, figure-hugging fashions that flattered her spare frame. Once, she famously posed in a Schiaparelli dress that the Surrealist artist Dalí had printed with a lobster—a symbol he used to signify sexuality. When the duke died in 1972, Simpson wore a waist-length chiffon veil and black Givenchy coat to the funeral, and, acid tongue still intact, couldn't help herself from criticizing the queen's dowdy ensemble.

Today, Simpson's defiant fashionability is still an inspiration. In 2011, Madonna directed a film about Simpson's life, called *W.E.*, which reinvigorated interest in the duchess's influence. But the designer Roland Mouret, whose 2011 collection included a dress named after Simpson, summed her up best: "We use clothes to erase our mistakes and to highlight what we like; Wallis is one of the best students of fashion school in that way."

Simpson, wearing the sort of elegant, fitted dress that was typical of her style.

3

Coco Chanel

FASHION

Modernizer

FULL NAME:
Gabrielle Chanel

BORN:
August 19, 1883, Saumur, France

OCCUPATION:
Fashion designer, couturier

BAD GIRL CRED:
Chanel's style was as shockingly unconventional
as her life. The inventor of how modern women
dress, she made comfort and simplicity radical.

It's a warm summer night in Moulins, and officers from the barracks have crowded into La Rotonde, a popular cabaret (nightclub) in this small French town. They're rowdily drinking beer, talking, and laughing with ladies wearing flouncy, elaborate dresses. Then the piano music starts. Most don't even look up at the slender eighteen-year-old brunette in the simple dress standing beside the piano—but she begins singing, bravely carrying a tune above the din of their voices:

> Qui qu'a qui qu'a vu Coco?
> Eh! Coco!
> Eh! Coco!
> Qui qu'a qui qu'a vu Coco?
> Eh! Coco!

Walk down a fancy shopping street in any city today and you'll surely see the two back-to-back C's that make up the Chanel logo. Today, Chanel may be one of the most coveted high-fashion brands, but it took Coco Chanel, the fashion house's founder, many years to establish its dominance. In her youth, when she sang a song about a lost dog named Coco, the orphan and seamstress had no idea that the nickname she'd wind up hating—"Coco" Chanel—would become the most powerful name in fashion.

LITTLE ORPHAN
Coco

Gabrielle Chanel's life did not begin in a promising way: she was born in a poorhouse in a market town called Saumur. Her parents were unmarried market traders who survived on limited means. By the time Chanel was eleven, her mother had died. Chanel's father, who was frequently absent, did not want to raise her, and instead drove her and her two sisters to Aubazine, to the Congregation of the Sacred Heart of Mary: an orphanage run by nuns.

Chanel's life at the orphanage was regimented, but not bad. She was surrounded by nuns who wore black robes and white linens, jade crosses and veils; the uniform for the orphans was black, too. But when Chanel turned fifteen, the nuns let her choose her own dress. She had a dressmaker create something clingy, in mauve, with a taffeta flounce at the bottom. Sadly, the nuns decided the dress was unfit for Chanel to wear to mass, and it was sent back.

At eighteen, Chanel—who didn't wish to become a nun—left the orphanage for the Notre Dame school in Moulins. She had already learned how to sew a little at the orphanage, and at the school she learned more. Soon, the mother superior of the school found Chanel a job at a cloth merchant, or draper's shop, where she was a shop assistant and seamstress. Chanel worked alongside her aunt Adrienne, who was close to her own age, and the two slept in an attic room above the shop. She also took on a second job on the weekends at a tailor's, where she modified clothes for soldiers. The soldiers took a shining to Chanel and Adrienne, who were both fetching young women, and began taking them out to La Rotonde, a popular cabaret. Chanel was determined to get on stage there, and finally, she did: in fact, she found herself a regular slot in the evening, performing two little ditties, "Ko Ko Ri Ko" and "Qui qu'a vu Coco."

A dressmaker's dummy. Previous page: Chanel in 1920.

FASHION SPOTLIGHT
Josephine Baker

FULL NAME:

Freda Josephine McDonald

BORN:

June 3, 1906, St. Louis, Missouri

OCCUPATION:

Dancer, civil rights activist

BAD GIRL CRED:

With sensual insouciance, Baker defied racism to make the stage her own.

Wildly gyrating on stage, frantically jiggling her behind in a move that almost resembled today's twerking, all while wearing nothing except for a skirt made of feathers—this was the dance that made Josephine Baker famous, and her image legendary. The "savage" dance may have defined that image, but her life was much more complex than this one memorable move.

Baker was born into a poor family, which meant she had to work from a young age. Starting at eight, she was employed by white families as a live-in domestic; it was a job where she was unappreciated, and sometimes abused. But she ran away at thirteen to start a new life. She had a couple of marriages, neither of which lasted but one of which landed her a new last name— Baker. And she started dancing in clubs. By the mid-1920s, her success had led her to New York City, where she became a chorus-line dancer at a popular club in Harlem.

Baker's big break came when she moved to Paris in 1925. At the time, Paris was obsessed with American jazz, and Baker began dancing in La Revue Nègre at the Théâtre des Champs-Elysées. When she performed the Danse Sauvage ("savage dance") in her feather skirt (and no top!), the crowd went wild. The performance was topped only by her dance the following year, called La Folie du Jour, in which she performed in a skirt made of bananas. Her wild popularity found her famous friends, such as the great Cubist artist Pablo Picasso and the novelist Ernest Hemingway, and she earned the nickname "Black Venus." Though she was known for her erotic sensuality and wild costumes onstage, offstage she adopted a polished persona, and dressed in couture from designers like Chanel, Dior, and Balenciaga.

In 1936, Baker headed back to the United States to perform for the Ziegfeld Follies. After living in France, which was relatively racially integrated and tolerant, she was shocked by the hateful, racist response she got in her home country. Even *Time* magazine referred to her as a "Negro wench." And so she returned to France, where she worked for the French Resistance against the Nazis during World War II. Postwar, when Baker would tour the U.S., she explicitly refused to perform for segregated audiences, using her popularity as a tool in the fight for black civil rights. She continued her advocacy into her old age, and passed away at age sixty-eight, four days after a huge performance bankrolled by Prince Rainier and Princess Grace of Monaco, along with Jacqueline Kennedy Onassis.

Today, Baker's influence is every-where. Rihanna's shocking see-through dress and skullcap at the 2014 CFDA (Council of Fashion Designers of America) Fashion Awards were a nod to Baker; so too was Beyoncé's performance at Fashion Rocks in 2006, where she did the banana dance in her own banana skirt. In 2011, Prada's collection was a tribute to the dancer, featuring banana-print clothing modeled by beautiful black women with hair styled in curls like Baker's. Mostly, though, Baker paved the way for sensual, stylish women of color to seize the limelight—her refusal to be judged is her lasting legacy.

Baker in 1926, looking sassy in her banana skirt.

LOVE
as a Muse

Chanel in 1928, wearing a nautical jersey and trousers.

When she was twenty-one, Chanel met Étienne Balsan, a wealthy cavalry officer three years older than her. She ran away with him to his large house in the country, which he called Royallieu, and became his mistress. Royallieu was a palatial estate, complete with stables and servants, a world away from the orphanage of Chanel's childhood. Chanel rode the horses and took to wearing boyish riding clothes around the manor: breeches and jackets, which she had made by a local tailor. Compared to the long dresses, corsets, and elaborate hats the other women at Royallieu wore, Chanel's clothes were strange and daring.

Chanel's six years at Royallieu were influential for her. She was introduced to French society: she met socialites, famous actresses, and, importantly, Boy Capel. Despite the fact that she was Balsan's mistress, Chanel was smitten by Capel, a polo player who was also fabulously rich. They began a relationship, though, by all accounts,

Capel had relationships with other women at the same time. Perhaps frustrated, Chanel began to take Capel's tailored sporting clothes and cut them up, to modify them into something she could wear herself. And people took note of her unusual style.

Around the same time, Chanel began to experiment with making hats. Capel and Balsan (in an oddly co-operative arrangement, given that they both had romantic relationships with Chanel) agreed to share the cost of setting her up with a business: Balsan supplied an apartment in Paris for Chanel to work out of, and Capel paid the operating costs. And so Chanel became a milliner. At the time, hats for women were large and gaudy, covered in bows. Chanel's hats were simple straw pieces that were chic and unfussy, and her first clients—actresses she knew from Royallieu—made her designs popular.

Chanel's Paris business was so successful that she began to make clothes, too, often modeled after the sort of men's country clothing she'd adapted for herself: sleek and tailored, and definitively without a corset. She opened another shop, in Deauville, a fashionable seaside town, in 1913, and retreated there when World War I broke out the following year.

CORSETS

Corsets defined the silhouette of women's fashion beginning in the sixteenth century. Designed to cinch the waist to make it smaller, a corset is usually made with a stiff material (historically, reed or whalebone) and laced up in the back to give women a shapely, hourglass figure that was seen as feminine (accentuating the breasts and hips). In trying to achieve the smallest waist possible, women sometimes laced their corsets so tightly they had difficulty breathing. Even when worn normally, corsets made it challenging for women to move around easily.

The lack of material at hand caused her to experiment, so she began cutting clothes from the sweaters of stable boys. These designs were a major success. Chanel took inspiration from the working class, and brought in elements like neckerchiefs, worn by stonemasons, and dungarees (overalls), worn by mechanics. But more important, Chanel's clothing was comfortable and easy to move around in—she designed the sort of things *she* wanted to wear. Because of its boyishness, her aesthetic became known as the "garçonne look" (*garçonne* means "boy" or "boyish" in French). It was exactly the sort of practical clothing that suited the climate of the Great War, and from 1914 to 1918 Chanel's business expanded. By 1919, she was well known as a couturier. For her, however, the decade would end in tragedy: that same year, her lover Boy Capel died in a car crash.

Reeling from Capel's death, Chanel took herself to the Côte d'Azur, a beach resort area in the south of France, to process her grief. There, she breathed in the smells of the coast: fresh air, flowers. And she decided to make a perfume. In 1920, she was introduced to Ernest Beaux, who formulated a number of perfumes for her; she chose number five. And so Chanel No. 5 was born. A complex scent featuring jasmine,

You may have seen this bottle on your grandma's bureau, but when Chanel No. 5 launched, it was groundbreaking and a little bit risqué.

ylang ylang, rose, and sandalwood, No. 5 broke the rules of women's perfumes. At the time, respectable ladies wore the scent of a single flower, while courtesans (mistresses, or sometimes prostitutes) favored the flower jasmine but also musk, an animal scent that comes from deer. Chanel No. 5 combined these: it was complex, layered, and unconventional. With this perfume and her tailored, tomboyish clothing, Chanel had defined both the aesthetic and the scent of the self-reliant women of the era.

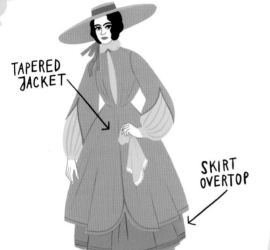

TAPERED
JACKET

SKIRT
OVERTOP

BLOOMER
PANTS

AMELIA BLOOMER

ICONIC LOOK № 3

For **AMELIA BLOOMER**, pants were a feminist statement. As the editor of the first newspaper for women, *The Lily* (published between 1849 and 1853), she was a strong advocate for women's rights, and when she first encountered the idea of pants for women, she was immediately sold. She enthusiastically promoted this new fashion in *The Lily*, and when it was featured in other publications, it was given her name: bloomers.

BACK *in* BLACK

Chanel at work in 1937.

Soon after, Chanel debuted another innovation: the little black dress. A short, streamlined number, it was called "Chanel's Ford" by *Vogue* magazine because, like Ford's Model T car, it was meant to be accessible to all classes. It was an equalizer: no longer were women expected to wear a gaudy, frilly, expensive dress to look classy. Riding on these successful innovations, by the '30s Chanel was at the peak of her career, employing four thousand people and running five boutiques. Her life could not have been more removed from the one she had lived at the orphanage.

Chanel continued to experiment; one of her most grandiose adventures was in Hollywood, where in 1930 Samuel Goldwyn gave her an unprecedented $1 million to design costumes for his movies. Though Chanel designed for two films, the relationship ultimately ended—Hollywood was looking for something flashier. Unperturbed, she returned to Paris, where her designs for stage productions for people like Jean Cocteau (an edgy French writer, artist, and filmmaker) were popular.

World War II broke out in Europe in 1939. And even though Paris's fashion industry was blind at first to the war's repercussions, Chanel closed her business that September. "This is no time for fashion," she said. When the Nazis occupied Paris in 1940, Chanel moved into the Ritz Hotel. By 1941, she had begun an affair with Hans Günther von Dincklage, a German officer she'd met a few years earlier in Paris. This relationship had dire repercussions for Chanel: when Paris was liberated in 1944, she was accused of being a Nazi collaborator. She was protected from prosecution, but postwar France was suspicious of her, and she retreated to Switzerland.

COCO'S MEN

Unlike most women of her era, Chanel never married, and she had love affairs with many men. Several became muses for her designs, and some Chanel supported artistically. They included:

The Duke of Westminster: Hugh Grosvenor, son of the Earl of Grosvenor, and the wealthiest man in Britain. During their ten-year relationship, Chanel opened up shop in London and began making clothes with a more formal edge, to suit British tastes.

Hans Günther von Dincklage: A Nazi officer with whom Chanel had an affair. Their relationship spurred rumors that Chanel was a Nazi collaborator.

Grand Duke Dmitri Pavlovich: A Russian royal who escaped the 1917 revolution. Chanel's relationship with him led to her experiments with patterns taken from Russian folklore.

Paul Iribe: A talented fashion illustrator who was controversial for his French nationalist politics. He collapsed and died while playing tennis with Chanel.

Igor Stravinsky: A daring composer to whom Chanel offered financial support. Many believed the two had an affair.

Pierre Reverdy: An avant-garde poet Chanel fell in love with and funded; his poetry and devotion to art influenced her.

Étienne Balsan: A rich playboy who introduced Chanel to French society and its ways of dressing.

Boy Capel: A wealthy polo player whose sportswear partially inspired Chanel's designs.

It's 1947, and in Paris the streets are busy with happy shoppers. Women sashay along the sidewalks, all with the same silhouette: a full skirt, soft shoulders, and a tiny, corseted waist. Hourglass figures, every one, traditional and ladylike. It's the so-called New Look from designer Christian Dior, the signature feature of which is a return to traditional values and femininity. Chanel stands to the side and observes. She says, with bitterness in her voice, "Look how ridiculous these women are, wearing clothes by a man who doesn't know women, never had one, and dreams of being one."

In 1947, Christian Dior, a promising young designer, was given the job of revitalizing the Parisian fashion industry. He did so with what he called the New Look, which revived the ideals of traditional femininity from the Victorian era: women were back in corsets again, in a major way. Dior's fashions offered comfort to people in the postwar era, indulging their nostalgia for less complicated times—times when women mostly stayed at home and attended to domestic tasks. But the New Look threw aside all of Chanel's revolutionary ideas about dressing; fashion for women was no longer about being comfortable and free to move about. And, no surprise, Chanel absolutely hated it. She viewed Dior's designs with open malice, and made nasty comments about them to the press. Finally, unable to take it any longer, she emerged from retirement in 1954, at age seventy-one, to go to war with Dior over the reigning fashion of the era.

CHANEL

THE BIG
Comeback

When Chanel's new collection debuted, the initial response was not what she had hoped for. Chanel's fresh designs played on all her ideals from the past, but French and English reviewers saw them as a throwback, rather than as revolutionary. One newspaper referred to the collection as a "sad retrospective"; most others seemed to agree. However, Chanel fared better in the U.S., where a more casual style ruled and people approved of her comfortable designs.

There, a Chanel suit became a marker of elegance. Chanel, in fact, became the go-to designer for Hollywood celebrities—and soon politicians, too, as Jackie Kennedy, the fashion-conscious First Lady married to President John F. Kennedy, favored couture, including Chanel. Famously, Jackie was wearing a bright pink Chanel suit the day JFK was assassinated in 1963.

Chanel never stopped working. In fact, the day before she died, Chanel was attending to her new couture collection, attempting to finish it. Feeling tired, she went to bed early, and passed away the next day, January 10, 1971. She was eighty-seven. Her maid dressed her in an immaculate white suit and blouse, and at her funeral, her coffin was covered in an enormous display of white flowers. A Who's Who of designers and fashion models attended the ceremony to pay their respects to the woman who had changed fashion forever. Two weeks after her death, her final collection debuted—and the crowd gave a standing ovation. It was the end of an era.

Today, Chanel's legacy lingers. The little black dress, the Chanel suit, and casual, uncorseted clothes—if Chanel hadn't created these, it's hard to imagine where fashion would be today. Out of all Chanel's ideas, the one that is most obvious in today's womenswear is simplicity and comfortable elegance. Perhaps she said it best herself: "Fashion fades, only style remains the same."

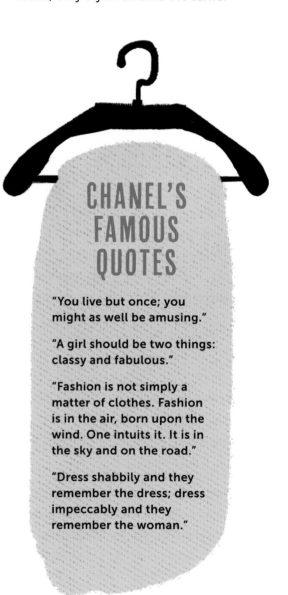

CHANEL'S FAMOUS QUOTES

"You live but once; you might as well be amusing."

"A girl should be two things: classy and fabulous."

"Fashion is not simply a matter of clothes. Fashion is in the air, born upon the wind. One intuits it. It is in the sky and on the road."

"Dress shabbily and they remember the dress; dress impeccably and they remember the woman."

FASHION SPOTLIGHT
Louise Brooks

FULL NAME:
Mary Louise Brooks

BORN:
November 14, 1906, Cherryvale, Kansas

OCCUPATION:
Actress, dancer

BAD GIRL CRED:
**The archetypal flapper, Brooks
embodied bohemian liberation.**

If you picture a 1920s flapper, with a bobbed haircut, a drop-waist dress, a cloche hat, and an insolent look, the image in your mind is likely to resemble Louise Brooks (nicknamed "Lulu"). One of the first rebellious female film stars, Brooks was an icon of the liberal 1920s in both her fashion and her lifestyle.

Brooks had a lonely childhood. Though her family lived comfortably in a remote town in Kansas, her parents were too self-absorbed to pay much attention to her, and she was largely neglected. "Any squalling brats [we] produce [can] take care of themselves," her mother commented. When she was only nine, Brooks went through a trauma that left an indelible mark on her life: she was sexually assaulted by a neighbor. She never regarded men with trust after that.

Perhaps because of her parents' neglect, Brooks always yearned for attention, and took to performance at a young age. At fifteen, she left home to join an avant-garde dance troupe in Los Angeles, where she remade herself into a stylish dancing girl. She was fired from the troupe in 1922 but soon made her way into the Ziegfeld Follies, a famous theatrical company in New York. Working with the Follies meant that Brooks made wealthy and fashionable friends, and it also quickly got her noticed: first, by a producer for Paramount Pictures, and second, by Charlie Chaplin, a celebrated comedic actor. She had a fling with Chaplin that first summer. Soon after, her powerful connections paid off, and she began starring in films. She was cast as the lead in silent films such as *A Girl in Every Port*, and her bobbed hair started a craze. "A well dressed woman, even though her purse is painfully empty, can conquer the world," she said. And she certainly did.

Brooks became known for her lifestyle as much as for her looks. She had a series of romances with men, but never anything lasting, and she never had children. She lived up to the flappers' reputation as hard-drinking, promiscuous, and self-righteous, and she swanned around in wide-legged trousers, silk blouses, furs, and pearls. To maintain her sleek flapper form, she didn't wear a bra. Women imitated her bold style, and she even became the inspiration for a flapper cartoon strip called *Dixie Dugan*. Most notoriously, in 1929 she relocated to Germany, where she starred in a film called *Pandora's Box*. Her character, Lulu, was wildly uninhibited and sexual; at the time, this was quite shocking, and it also gave Brooks a memorable nickname.

Brooks returned to Hollywood, but after she turned down a high-profile role in *The Public Enemy* (to visit her boyfriend), she stopped getting booked, and her hard-drinking lifestyle took its toll. Her career stalled until the '50s, when French film historians rediscovered her and declared her one of film's icons. Ever the contrarian, she took it all with a grain of salt, shrugging off the attention. She passed away in 1985 at age seventy-eight.

Brooks in 1926, posing in typical flapper garb.

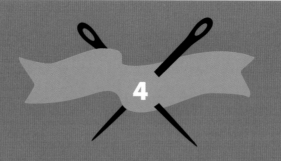

Frida Kahlo

FASHION

Artist

FULL NAME:
Magdalena Carmen Frieda Kahlo y Calderón

BORN:
July 6, 1907, Mexico City

OCCUPATION:
Artist

BAD GIRL CRED:
One of the twentieth century's greatest painters,
Frida turned her image and body into a
provocative statement.

A family gathers in a sunny Mexico City courtyard for a portrait, taken by the family patriarch. Everyone is dressed to the nines; the men are in three-piece suits and the women are in tidy dresses. All except one, that is: a mischievous-looking, dark-eyed teenage girl who stands to the side, posing with insouciant bravado. Her dark hair is slicked back and parted, and she wears a well-tailored three-piece men's suit, in gray. She looks like a boy, and she looks like she's ready for anything.

Even when she was young, Frida Kahlo was never interested in blending in, and she continued to provoke throughout her life. The Mexican artist and socialist, familiar for her self-portraits complete with luxurious unibrow and colorful and eclectic fashions, was a force to be reckoned with. Her powerful art and iconoclastic image still inspire mimicry today.

THE ARTIST AS A
Young Woman

Frida Kahlo claimed that she was born the year of the Mexican Revolution, 1910. It's a poetic idea, and one that adds to her mystique—but the clever and mischievous artist was actually born three years earlier and raised in the picturesque town of Coyoacán (now a suburb of Mexico City). Her childhood was idyllic until age six, when she caught polio, which deformed her right leg, causing it to be thinner than her left. In order to hide it, she started wearing ankle-length skirts and pants. But in this case, and for the rest of her life, her physical problems never prevented her from pursuing life with absolute gusto. She was the older of two girls, and her German-born father's favorite. A photographer by trade, he doted on her and encouraged her, pinning all the family's academic and professional hopes on Kahlo the way families of the era usually did with their eldest boy.

Perhaps partially due to her father's encouragement, Kahlo was strong-willed and nonconformist from a young age. By fourteen, she was wearing her hair like a flapper: a short crop, with blunt-cut bangs straight across her forehead. In 1922, her parents enrolled her in an elite preparatory school where she was one of only thirty-five girls, and although her school had no uniform, she turned up looking like a German high school student, in a pleated skirt, stockings, boots, and a black straw hat. She often dressed like a boy and would ride a bike around her neighborhood wearing blue coveralls, usually with a group of boys, and carried a boy's knapsack to school.

Taken aback by her unfeminine appearance, local mothers would exclaim, "What an ugly girl!" But Kahlo didn't care. In her opinion, most of the girls at her school were *"cursi"* (silly and cheesy). Instead of trying to fit in with these classmates, she banded together instead with a group of brainy misfits—boys and girls more like herself. Together, they ran amok and

played many pranks—including riding a donkey through the school halls and lighting firecrackers during a renowned professor's lecture. Defiant of authority, Kahlo made fun of the muralists who had been hired to paint various parts of the school. Among them was Diego Rivera, one of Mexico's most famous painters, whose murals documented the 1910 revolution and championed socialist ideals. While he was up painting the walls, she'd taunt him from the ground, calling him "Old Fatso." The rumor goes that at that moment, she developed a huge crush on the famous painter.

A section from Diego Rivera's mural *Dream of a Sunday Afternoon in Alameda Central Park* (1947). You can find Frida Kahlo in this painting—fourth from the left in a purple shawl.
Opposite: Kahlo as a young girl.
Previous page: A graffiti artist's take on Kahlo.

A life-changing tragedy struck Kahlo at age eighteen on the way to school. Her bus collided with a streetcar, and, in horrifying slow motion, a metal rod pierced her body, breaking many of her bones and damaging organs, including her uterus. Her prognosis wasn't good, but in the end, Kahlo survived. It took her a great deal of time to recover, but while she was confined to bed, Kahlo began to paint, using a small easel on her lap. She hung a mirror from her bed's canopy, and in this way she was able to use herself as a subject for her paintings.

SOCIALISM & COMMUNISM

Socialism and communism are political systems that aim for equality within society. Socialists believe the economy and essential services (like hospitals and schools) should be managed by the state. Communism goes one step further, stripping away class distinctions and pay differences, as well as many freedoms. In the early twentieth century, both philosophies were growing in popularity, and organizations within many countries hoped for revolution.

THE ELEPHANT
and the Dove

Kahlo and Rivera, 1932.

A man stands on a scaffold, twenty feet off the ground. He holds a paintbrush, and in careful, confident strokes, he paints the wall in front of him ... until, he hears a voice calling. "Diego!" Seeing the girl below him—eighteen years old, with long, dark hair and thick eyebrows that meet above her nose—the painter, Diego Rivera, climbs down to the ground. "I'd like you to look at my paintings," she says. "Will you?"

"Yes," the man replies, and follows her.

"I'm worried about what you'll tell me," the young woman says as he inspects the paintings. "I've heard that if a pretty girl asks, you'll always encourage her. But I want to know the truth. Should I be a painter?"

"In my honest opinion, no matter what stands in your way, you must paint," he tells her.

The girl says that she has other paintings to show him. She gives him her address, and finishes with, "My name is Frida Kahlo."

And then the man realizes who she is. "I remember you!" he exclaims.

"Yes, I'm the girl who taunted you," she says merrily. And she leaves.

After the fateful day that Kahlo beckoned Rivera down to look at her paintings, the two started to become friends. Around the same time, Kahlo joined the Young Communist League. She changed the way she dressed to suit her rabble-rousing frame of mind, adopting red and black shirts, blue jeans, and leather jackets adorned with a hammer-and-sickle pin—the Communist emblem. It was the outfit of a revolutionary. Seeing her this way, Diego Rivera painted her into one of his murals that celebrated socialism, depicting her wearing a red shirt and handing out weapons to revolutionaries. One thing led to another, and soon the two were lovers, despite the fact that he was nearly twenty years older than her. They married in 1929. They made a strange pair: she twenty-two, he forty-two, she five foot three and one hundred pounds, and he six feet and three hundred pounds. Kahlo's mother compared it to the marriage of an elephant and a dove.

After Rivera and Kahlo married, she undertook a more dramatic style transformation. Kahlo adopted the Tehuana costume, a style of dress that had emerged in Tehuantepec, a city in the Mexican southeast. She'd always used clothing as a kind of language to communicate her state of mind, but

COMMUNIST STYLE

In the 1920s, communism was still new to the world—Russia only became a communist country in 1917, and the darker side of its totalitarian system of government hadn't yet become obvious. Many artists and intellectuals, in particular, were drawn to the romantic idea of a workers' revolution. Communism championed the common people, so communist revolutionaries tended to dress and act like the working class, even if they hadn't been born into it.

Kahlo wrapped in a *rebozo*.

Kahlo may have been drawn to the Tehuana costume because the region was famed for its matriarchal society: though men held political power, the women of Tehuantepec were known for their bold attitudes and their strength as breadwinners. But she also dressed this way to impress Rivera. As an avowed communist, he championed the worker and the Mexican people, and this traditional costume aligned Kahlo with the "real" Mexico rather than its colonial upper class. The Tehuana costume became synonymous with Kahlo's identity; in some of her later paintings, she would paint it, empty, to symbolize her presence (or absence).

During the early years of Kahlo and Rivera's marriage, her art style truly began to take form. She usually painted stylized self-portraits heavily influenced by Mexican indigenous history and filled with surreal symbolism. Clothing and costume figured heavily in Kahlo's paintings, various outfits suggesting backstories for her favorite character: herself.

this particular change was an important one, for it shaped her identity for years to come. To look like a Tehuana, Kahlo donned a *huipil* top (an embroidered tunic) and dramatic, floor-length skirts, underneath which she wore petticoats that she embroidered with bawdy Mexican sayings. She piled on jewelry, often handmade pieces in the style favored by Mexican Native people. She finished the look with a *rebozo*, a traditional Mexican scarf draped around her shoulders. She braided her hair, and sometimes wove ribbons and flowers into it.

FASHION SPOTLIGHT
Miuccia Prada

FULL NAME:

Miuccia Prada

BORN:

May 10, 1949, Milan, Italy

OCCUPATION:

Fashion designer

BAD GIRL CRED:

**Prada designs clothes to be interesting for women—
not pleasing to men.**

In a way, Miuccia Prada was born into fashion. In 1913, her grandfather launched the family business—a shop that sold suitcases, trunks, and bags. Initially successful, that business had grown stagnant by the time Miuccia was born, but Miu Miu (that was her nickname) would change all that.

Prada was always creative; by age fifteen, she was rebelling against her Catholic-school uniform of pleated skirts and brown shoes by incorporating the color pink into her wardrobe. Around the same time, miniskirts made by Mary Quant were taking young women's closets by storm. Prada's conservative parents didn't let her get anywhere near the thigh-baring skirts, but she took matters into her own hands, buying Salvation Army skirts and hemming them herself with a needle and thread before she went out at night.

She always wanted to go to art school, but it wasn't to be; her parents considered it too bohemian. But Prada, again, got where she wanted to go by taking an unexpected path: she enrolled in theater school at Milan's Piccolo Teatro, where she studied miming. She took it seriously, and mimed for six years. But she did more than just mime: at the same time, she studied political science at the State University of Milan, which was famous for its subversive student body. It wasn't long before Prada was a card-carrying member of the Italian Communist Party.

Prada wasn't a typical communist. She refused to don the usual wardrobe of blue jeans and button-down shirts, considering these requirements ridiculous. Instead, she continued to wear bohemian-inspired but definitely well-made ensembles by respected (but still edgy) French fashion designers such as Yves Saint Laurent and Pierre Cardin. The story of Prada, clad in designer fashions, handing out pamphlets at Communist rallies, has become legendary.

Eventually, Prada took over the family business, and transformed it from a sleepy and somewhat unknown firm to a global fashion power-house. As she had no formal fashion education, her designs were always considered unconventional. A feminist as well as a communist, Prada made clothing intended to be interesting to women rather than pleasing to men. She is credited with making "ugly" fashionable, and regularly created clothing in unusual, sometimes ill-fitting shapes, and in strange colors, like brownish purple and soup green. "I think probably people confuse fashion with being beautiful or being sexy or attractive," she says. "Very often people use it as a [tool], not as pleasure."

Though the modern Prada is a multimillion-dollar company, Miuccia Prada has held on to her youthful communist sentiments. A 2014 collection that incorporated art from around the world was inspired by Diego Rivera's political murals.

A modern version of the iconic Prada bag.

DOUBLE
Trouble

Two identical dark-haired women sit in chairs, side by side, holding hands. The woman on the left wears a lacy white Victorian wedding dress; the woman on the right, a colorful Tehuana costume with a green skirt and royal blue top. The woman on the right holds a locket with a photo of a young Diego Rivera in it, and a small vein running from the locket connects the hearts of the two women. The heart of the woman in the Tehuana costume is whole. The heart of the woman in the white dress is broken. The woman in the white dress holds a pair of scissors, which she uses to cut the vein, and she bleeds onto her dress, helplessly.

This painting is called *The Two Fridas*. Painted by Kahlo after her divorce from Rivera in 1939, it was meant to symbolize the Kahlo that Rivera loved (in the Tehuana dress) and the Kahlo that he didn't (in the white dress). Rivera and Kahlo's marriage had been problematic right from the beginning. Even before he met Kahlo, Rivera was known as a womanizer who regularly cheated on his romantic partners. After he married Kahlo, he continued to philander, and she reacted angrily and loudly. The two famously maintained separate houses connected by a bridge, a measure to help them get along a little better. However, Rivera pushed Kahlo too far in 1934, when she discovered his affair with her sister, Cristina. Heartbroken, Kahlo briefly gave up wearing her beloved Tehuana dresses and cut her hair short, but she continued her relationship with Rivera.

The Two Fridas, 1939.

The affair changed her, though: she became more complicated, more self-righteous, and she began to dabble on the side herself, with both men and women. One of Kahlo's most notorious love affairs was with the famous Russian socialist Leon Trotsky, who took refuge in Mexico in 1936; some think Rivera's discovery of the affair was the reason for the couple's 1939 divorce. Prior to their separation, Kahlo traveled to Paris for an exhibition of her work (along with the work of other Mexican artists), where she supposedly became romantically involved with the dancer Josephine Baker. Upon returning home, she and Rivera formally divorced, but it didn't last long: they remarried in 1940, mutually agreeing that they were better together than apart, despite their problems.

Though her personal life was tumultuous, Kahlo's creative successes began to flourish around this time. She exhibited her art in both New York (1938) and Paris (1939) to great acclaim, and *Vogue* magazine ran a feature on her, with a photo of Kahlo's jewelry-laden hand on the cover. The fashion world took note of the artist's signature style; after her stint in Paris, where Kahlo's Tehuana dress captured the attention of fashion-conscious Parisians, edgy designer Elsa Schiaparelli debuted a dress called *La Robe Madame Rivera*.

Sirens wailing, an ambulance, accompanied by a motorcycle escort, pulls up outside of the Galeria Arte Contemporáneo in Mexico City in the spring of 1953. The crowd inside the gallery turns to watch as attendants pull a bed out of the ambulance, hold it aloft, and carry it inside the gallery, where colorful paintings line the walls. Everybody stares at the woman in the canopied bed: her dark hair is twisted into an updo, and she wears a traditional Mexican dress and heavy jewelry. There are rings on all of her fingers and her nails are painted. The bed itself is adorned with religious figurines, pictures of politicians and artists, and paintings; it smells strongly of Schiaparelli's Shocking! *perfume.*

By the mid-'40s, Kahlo's health was getting worse. The effects of her childhood polio and streetcar accident continued to plague her. She had several pregnancies that couldn't be carried to term because of her damaged uterus, and she wore plaster corsets throughout her life to support her weak spine. She decorated these, painting them with wild creatures like tigers and birds and political symbols like hammers and sickles—private embellishments to make an ugly part of her life beautiful. By the '50s, she had undergone a series of bone grafts and was mostly bedridden, but she still dressed in her own flamboyant way, appearing ready for a fiesta at any moment. And she did have an occasion to party at her 1953 solo show, at which she made a triumphant appearance, carried in on a bed. Only a few months later, she developed gangrene in her leg, and it was amputated below the knee. Physically weakened, she passed away the following year at age forty-seven.

Kahlo's influence in art and fashion was immense. She was an icon of rebellion whose wild life reads like a playbook for how to live and dress like an artist. Kahlo has inspired a slew of modern fashion designers, including Jean Paul Gaultier, who in 1998 launched a collection entirely based on her clothes. A 2002 biopic starring Salma Hayek reignited the public's interest in Kahlo's life. Still, the best representation of Kahlo's revolutionary style is in her art.

Clockwise from bottom left: Kahlo, during a shoot for *Vogue* in 1937; Kahlo's image is everywhere—she's even become graffiti; Salma Hayek playing Kahlo in the 2002 film *Frida*; Kahlo's painting *Memory, the Heart*, from 1937.

ICONIC LOOK № 4

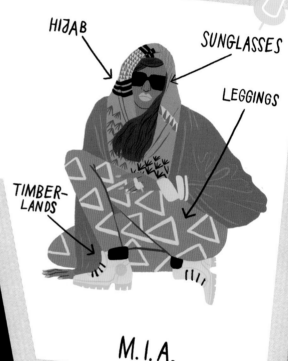

HIJAB

SUNGLASSES

LEGGINGS

TIMBER-LANDS

M.I.A.

Grammy-winning, politically radical musician **M.I.A.** has often used her image as propaganda art for her beliefs. The daughter of a revolutionary from the militant Tamil Tigers political group in Sri Lanka, she has worked tigers into her album art. Her clothing often draws from world cultures, defying the dominance of Western fashions. One of her most controversial outfits, which she wore to an awards show, was a burqa—a long, draping garment some Muslim women wear to cover their face and body—printed with the art for her album *Kala*. More often, her look draws equally from street fashion and global culture.

FASHION SPOTLIGHT
Elsa Schiaparelli

FULL NAME:

Elsa Luisa Maria Schiaparelli

BORN:

September 10, 1890, Rome, Italy

OCCUPATION:

Fashion designer

BAD GIRL CRED:

**Schiaparelli broke design boundaries
by fusing fashion with art.**

Shocking! was Elsa Schiaparelli's perfume. It was named after her signature color, shocking pink, but the name also reflected the unorthodox designer's life and clothing, both of which would have made an uptight person grit their teeth.

Schiaparelli (nicknamed Schiap) always did things her own way. Her upper-class Italian family made no bones about the fact that they had wanted a boy, and told her that she was ugly. Though these comments hurt her, they also pushed her to rebel. After high school she studied philosophy at the University of Rome and, while there, published a book of poetry that was so provocatively sexy that her parents sent her to a convent. Having none of it, Schiap went on a hunger strike. As soon as the convent freed her, she ran away to London, where she became a nanny.

Nannying was a dull job for the rebellious Schiaparelli, so for excitement, she started going to society balls dressed in cutting-edge dresses she designed herself. She met a man and married him, then relocated to New York, where she gave birth to a daughter. While there, she began working at a fashion boutique—and when her marriage fell apart, fashion was the love she chose. She moved to Paris, took a loan from a friend, and began making clothes. Her debut collection was inspired by Futurism—an early-twentieth-century artistic movement that celebrated technology and modernity—and named "Display 1." It featured strange design details called *trompe l'œil* that tricked people into seeing patterns in 3D; one item, a sweater with a *trompe l'œil* bowtie, caught the eye of a *Paris Vogue* editor. Soon Schiaparelli's designs were in the magazine, and in the closets of the most fashionable artists and intellectuals.

When Schiaparelli first began designing, fashion was firmly tied to both beauty and practicality. One could buy a gorgeous couture dress or a comfortable, boyish ensemble. But what Schiaparelli brought to fashion was flamboyant creativity and a firm belief that clothes were art. Her main competitor at the time was Coco Chanel. The two could not have been clearer opposites. Chanel's designs were all about practicality; Schiaparelli's were gloriously artistic, and often bizarre.

With an eye for the absurd, Schiaparelli began collaborating with artists. Her work with legendary Surrealist artists like Salvador Dalí and Jean Cocteau was fascinating and compelling, transforming fashion from mere clothing to collectors' pieces. The Dalí–Schiaparelli collaborations are the best known, including the Lobster Dress (famously worn by Wallis Simpson) and the Shoe Hat—which, as it sounds, was a hat shaped like a shoe.

Sadly, Schiaparelli didn't adapt to the changing times after World War II, and she shut down her fashion house in 1954. While she doesn't have the same sort of name recognition today as her rival Coco Chanel, Schiaparelli's ingenious designs forever changed the way people looked at clothes. And her name still has cachet: there's a NARS lipstick named after her (in shocking pink, of course), and in 2013, the brand was relaunched by an Italian businessman, Diego Della Valle, to much public interest. Her collaborations with artists predated by many years the way fashion today is viewed as a creative outlet. Thanks to Schiaparelli, fashion is art.

The famous Lobster Dress, designed by Schiaparelli and Dalì in 1937.

Marlene Dietrich

FASHION

Gender-Bender

FULL NAME:
Marie Magdalene Dietrich

BORN:
December 27, 1901, Schöneberg, Germany

OCCUPATION:
Actress, singer

BAD GIRL CRED:
Mixing femme-fatale glamour and masculine
attitude (and clothes), Dietrich redefined what
a sex symbol could be.

A beautiful woman moves slowly across the stage as the crowd cheers. She wears a tailcoat and a top hat, and she smokes languidly, gazing across the room. Two men and two women sit at a table; one of them wears a glittering dress. The woman in the suit descends from the stage, walks over to the table, and confidently lifts a flower from behind the ear of the woman in the shimmering gown. "May I have this?" she asks. The other woman agrees. And then, the woman in the tuxedo does something unexpected: she leans in and gives the other woman a sensual kiss, full on the lips. The crowd cheers, and the woman in the suit tips her top hat, grinning.

It may sound a little racy, but this is a scene from the movie *Morocco*, which isn't even from the twenty-first century: it was filmed in 1930, and was shot in black and white. About the love affair between a cabaret singer and a soldier, it's mostly remembered for its scandalous woman-to-woman kiss and the tuxedo-wearing actress, whose name was Marlene Dietrich. Dietrich's sultry attitude and provocative wardrobe—she wore pants far before it was considered acceptable for women to do so—made her a legend.

BORN TO BE
Bad

Marlene Dietrich's childhood began in a fairly conventional way. When she was young, she attended private school and aspired to become a professional violinist. But as a teenager she quit music to become an actress; she went to film school and started to take small parts. To appease her family, who thought that acting was a tawdry career choice, she combined her first names to come up with her stage name: Marlene Dietrich.

In the early '20s as an actress in Berlin, Dietrich was hardworking, and also a little devious. She had a habit of not returning costumes for the parts

she played; the result was a packed wardrobe that made it easier for her to dress for a part. At one early casting call, she wore a pirate's hat, a dramatic velvet coat, and a monocle on one eye, and ended up landing the part of an observer in a courtroom. At her second casting call she auditioned for the role of a "girlfriend." Not knowing whether it was a respectable sort of girlfriend or not, Dietrich erred on the side of "or not," choosing a racy flapper dress and bright green gloves. The gloves attracted the attention of the director, Rudolf Sieber. He gave her the part, and, soon after, he proposed.

While Dietrich was with Sieber, she lived a carefree life, gallivanting around town in his roadster and admiring the transvestites (cross-dressing men) on street corners. She declared, brazenly, that "only the pansies know how to look like a sexy woman." ("Pansy" was a term used to refer to a gay man at that time, though it is considered derogatory now.) She and her husband went to the cabarets and hung around with transvestites there; Dietrich befriended them and offered them her style advice. To blend in better with her glamorous cross-dressing friends, she had her husband's tailor make her a man's suit with a top hat and tails. She would put on that outfit—caring little that she wasn't dressed like any of the other women in the cabaret—and dance the night away.

Dietrich in *The Blue Angel* (previous page) and *Blonde Venus* (above).

SHE'S GOT
Legs

Dietrich's mother, concerned about her daughter's wild lifestyle, encouraged her to have children. In 1924, Dietrich took her mother's advice and gave birth to a baby girl, Maria Elisabeth Sieber. However, having a child did little to curb her desire to experience life and perform. By 1926, she was right back to work. In 1929, she had her big break—in a film called *The Blue Angel*, directed by Josef von Sternberg, who then claimed to have "discovered" her (though she'd been an actress for years). In *The Blue Angel*, Dietrich played a nightclub singer called Lola Lola who seduces—and destroys the life of—a schoolteacher. She wore a dress with a dramatic (and, at the time, very risqué) slit up the side, which made her legs famous; they were reportedly insured for a million dollars. From that point on, Dietrich was cast as a seductress, in similar roles to those of another big-screen siren, Greta Garbo—who was also European, and even looked like Dietrich.

Soon after *The Blue Angel*, Dietrich was cast in *Morocco*, the sultry film in which she wore a suit and kissed another woman on the lips. Her wardrobe for *Morocco* was designed, with her input, by costumer Travis Banton. Dressing her in a suit not only teased audiences, who wanted to see her famous legs again and were intrigued by the image of this femme fatale in menswear, but also played into her long-held preference for wearing men's clothes. "I'm sincere in my preference for men's clothes—I do not wear them to be sensational," she said of her taste for trousers. And, indeed, despite the influence of Chanel and her "garçonne look," it was very unusual for a woman to wear trousers in the 1930s (though some lesbians wore them as a way to express their sexuality). It could be that the only reason Dietrich got away with it was because her character was both a nightclub entertainer and one in an "exotic" country (Morocco) to boot. Dietrich's image was one of the first of a woman in a suit. It was beguiling, and remained influential for decades to come.

LESBIAN FASHION

For most of history, lesbians (and gay men) have experienced harsh discrimination, and sometimes violence, for loving people who are the same gender as them. Because of that, they had to keep their sexual preferences secret—while somehow showing potential romantic partners that they might be interested. Some lesbians did this with clothing: they would wear clothes that were more often associated with men, such as trousers. Since Dietrich was rumored to be bisexual, some of her clothing choices may have been very intentional signals, or else inspired by the lesbians she admired.

As she explored different fashions, Dietrich also explored different relationships. Her marriage to Sieber was a platonic one, and Dietrich was known for taking lovers both male and female, which only added to her gender-bending allure. One of Dietrich's most scandalous rumored affairs was with her lookalike, Greta Garbo—though whether the affair is truth or simply another part of the myth of Marlene Dietrich is impossible to prove. Regardless, her reputation stuck with her. When she was replaced in one film by another actress, Tallulah Bankhead, Bankhead quipped: "I always did want to get into Dietrich's pants."

FASHION SPOTLIGHT
George Sand

FULL NAME:
Amantine-Lucile-Aurore Dupin

BORN:
July 1, 1804, Paris, France

OCCUPATION:
Writer

BAD GIRL CRED:
**George Sand chose the name—
and life—of a man.**

It's not immediately obvious when glancing at the cover of any of George Sand's books that this celebrated nineteenth-century French writer was, in fact, a woman. If you were to travel back in time and meet her, you'd likely have the same reaction. At a time when women were expected to be subservient and docile, Sand was independent and confident, and boldly made a place for herself in the world. And she did much of it while dressed like a man.

Sand's habit of pushing the boundaries of female decorum began when she was a teenager. Then, Sand was known by her real name: Aurore Dupin. The young Sand enjoyed riding the French countryside on horseback, and, as some women did at that time, she wore men's clothes (riding coat, breeches) while doing it. It was simply more comfortable. But Sand took things further: rather than just wearing men's clothes, she pretended to *be* a man. She once wrote triumphantly in a letter to a friend about how, after riding to a nearby town, she had flirted with a local girl who likely considered her an eligible bachelor.

Despite her nontraditional leanings, Sand got married when she was eighteen and had two children. But rather than acting the meek wife, she hung around with a group of local bohemians, many of whom were men. To blend in better, she recommended her habit of wearing men's clothes: a blouse and trousers. It was an expression of her desire to move about freely in the world without the restrictions and expectations of proper behavior that were imposed on women. Soon, marriage itself began to hold Sand back, and she negotiated an arrangement with her husband—very unusual at the time—in which she would spend several months at a time in Paris while he remained in the countryside. In 1835, they got a legal separation, which allowed Sand to begin a series of romantic affairs (for which she's as famous as she is for her novels).

In Paris, Sand began to play with gender roles in earnest. In order to accompany her friends to cultural events where women could sit only in restricted areas, she cross-dressed. She wore a thick, gray military coat with matching trousers and a vest, a cravat, and a hat; on her feet she wore heavy boots that were good for walking along the uneven Parisian streets. Dressed like this, Sand could go where she pleased and see Parisian society from all angles. Since she had taken up writing to support herself, her observations served as inspiration for her work as a novelist and journalist.

She first used the pen name George Sand for her second novel, *Indiana*, which featured a protagonist who wished for a world where women were free like men. Many saw the book as an overt criticism of marriage, while others thought it was about Sand herself. But the reason Sand chose a male pen name was simple: at the time, people believed that women writers wouldn't sell. Sand wasn't alone—other female writers were also using male pen names. But Sand, as always, took her androgynous dalliance one step further and began to use George Sand for her own name, too. As her work acquired both critical and popular acclaim, it was George Sand, not Aurore Dupin, who became famous. And so her transformation was complete: she was a woman with a man's name, a woman who wore men's clothes, and a woman who enjoyed many more freedoms in her life than other women alive at the same time. At her funeral, the Russian novelist Ivan Turgenev summed up her life neatly: "What a brave man she was, and what a good woman."

A woman with a man's name: George Sand at age 60, in 1864.

LET'S HEAR IT
for the Boys

In an army camp in Italy, a Jeep drives between tents adorned with roses, following signs showing only a drawing of shapely legs wearing garters. The Jeep stops in front of a stage, and a slender blonde wearing a floor-length strapless gown gingerly steps out: Marlene Dietrich. She ascends to the stage and begins to sing; the crowd of twenty thousand Allied soldiers cheers wildly. But then she stops suddenly, takes a piece of paper from a man in a uniform, and tears come to her eyes. She speaks slowly into her microphone: "Our boys have landed in Normandy!" The crowd erupts. It was D-Day—June 6, 1944.

Opposite: Dietrich, boosting the morale of American soldiers during World War II.

When World War II began, Marlene Dietrich was one of America's biggest film stars—and one who was born in Germany. Knowing her fame, the Nazi minister of propaganda, Joseph Goebbels, approached the blonde star to ask if she would consider returning to Germany to appear in films for the Reich. A staunch anti-Nazi, she flat-out refused, and became a U.S. citizen in 1939. As a cabaret performer with a good voice and a reputation as a sex symbol, she took an active role in the U.S. war effort, entertaining millions of troops who were at war in Europe.

Her campaigning went further than that, too. As part of the American propaganda effort, she recorded German versions of American pop songs, which were then broadcast for German soldiers to hear across enemy lines. Deeply affected by her work with soldiers, she worked hard to make the public back home care about the war.

For example, when she sat for a profile in *Vogue* magazine by the journalist Leo Lerman, she wore GI fatigues and lit cigarettes with a GI lighter made out of metal from airplanes, commenting, "The people over here must know that whatever we are doing will never be enough." Dietrich's army clothes were a provocative fashion statement; she knew her ensemble would get a mention in the magazine, and wanted to shake apathy on the home front by making the soldiers' plight relatable for women.

In her later years, Dietrich moved away from films and returned, again, to cabaret performance. She took her act to cities around the globe, including a notable run in Las Vegas, at the Sahara Hotel in 1953. The act was as much about her costumes as her songs: she became famous for wearing a see-through nude-colored dress that left very little to the imagination. But then, partway into the show, she would change into a top hat and tails and sing songs that were usually performed by men, including "I've Grown Accustomed to Her Face."

This was a song about being in love with a woman, and Dietrich didn't change the gender pronouns to "he" and "his" as most female singers would have done. Instead, she teased audiences with her ambiguous sexuality, and stepped into the role of the male singer. The manipulation of gender roles was classic Dietrich, and crowds ate it up. During her run at the Sahara, she was pulling in $30,000 U.S. per week—which in today's dollars would be over $250,000.

Dietrich's last film appearance was a cameo in the 1979 film *Just a Gigolo*, featuring glam rock star David Bowie. Seventy-eight-year-old Dietrich played the madam of a brothel where Bowie worked as a prostitute. In the film, Dietrich sang a sad, contemplative version of the popular song "Just a Gigolo"—originally a German cabaret song almost always sung by men, and thus the perfect note for Dietrich to go out on. She passed away at age ninety, but echoes of her gender-bending style live on. As recently as 2012, two different fashion designers debuted lines inspired by Dietrich at New York Fashion Week. In the end, her longevity comes down to her relentless pursuit of her own desires. As she famously said, "I dress for myself. Not for the image, not for the public, not for the fashion, not for men."

LE SMOKING

In 1966, the French designer Yves Saint Laurent debuted Le Smoking, a tailored tuxedo made for women. Even though Dietrich had worn tuxedos decades earlier, it wasn't until Le Smoking that suits for women really took off. In fact, even into the 1960s and '70s, women weren't allowed into nice hotels and restaurants if they were wearing those oh-so-inappropriate pants. Timing was everything. Le Smoking came out as the women's movement was gaining momentum, and liberated young women rallied to put on a well-made pair of pants.

Clockwise from top left: Dietrich in *Shanghai Express* (1932); posing in a dress in 1930; wearing her signature trousers in 1933.

ICONIC LOOK № 5

VELVET HAT

WHITE BUTTON-UP SHIRT

SILK TIE

BLACK VEST

MEN'S KHAKI TROUSERS

DIANE KEATON

DIANE KEATON brought a lot of herself to the role of Annie Hall in Woody Allen's 1977 film of the same name. That's no surprise: the movie was based on Diane and Woody's real-life relationship, and the character borrowed Diane's traits, from her nervousness to her intelligence. So when Diane brought her own clothes to set, Woody encouraged the costume designer to integrate them into the film. And so Annie Hall wore charmingly quirky menswear that made her stand out for what she was: a free spirit. In the feminist-powered '70s, Annie Hall was a hero, and her kooky ensembles became a trend that many adopted—the look of a strong woman, and one who has style.

FASHION SPOTLIGHT
Twiggy

FULL NAME:

Lesley Lawson (née Hornby)

BORN:

September 19, 1949, London, England

OCCUPATION:

Model

BAD GIRL CRED:

Boyish Twiggy opened the door for androgyny in fashion.

Hourglass curves, corsets, aprons, and cookies: in 1966, the housewife was still the feminine ideal. That was, until a skinny, knock-kneed teenager named Twiggy changed the image of womanhood forever.

Leslie Hornby was a boyishly thin seventeen-year-old when she was turned down for modeling in 1966; at five foot six, she was too short, she was told. But when she decided to participate as a hair model for the London celebrity hairdresser Leonard of Mayfair and had her hair cut into a short blonde crop, a photographer from the *Daily Express* newspaper spotted her, snapped her photo, and put it in the paper, declaring her "The Face of '66." From that point on, she was known as Twiggy, a variation on the nickname she'd had since she was small—Twigs, in reference to her slender build. Her modeling career quickly took off, and by 1967, she was boarding a flight for the United States, where she was greeted by a mob of reporters. The press dubbed her the biggest import since the Beatles, and the *New Yorker* used up close to a hundred pages covering her visit.

With her doe eyes, gangly limbs, and complete lack of womanly curves, Twiggy was precisely the opposite of the va-va-voom vixens and demure housewives of the past. She was awkward, she was youthful, and she captured the rebellious spirit of the time, when many young people were rejecting their parents' institutions. Though models today are often not very curvaceous, back then Twiggy's figure was considered unsexy—one fashion magazine, *Look*, captured the sentiment with the sarcastic headline "Is It a Girl? Is It a Boy? No, It's Twiggy." Twiggy was paving the way for androgynous beauty: she was considered beautiful even though she wasn't conventionally feminine, and was in fact somewhat boyish, echoing the boundary-pushing flappers of the 1920s.

Fashion photographers loved her because her frame was perfect for the youthful fashions of the era— by the late '60s, fashion had moved on from full skirts and pointed busts to miniskirts and A-line dresses. Designers experimented with so-called unisex fashions like jumpsuits, and boyish Twiggy was the one to model them. Photographers loved to cross-dress her, too: Twiggy in a suit was a common sight.

Today, Twiggy is controversial. Because she was so skinny, she became an inspirational figure for girls with body-image issues, and some blame the popularity of very thin models like her for eating disorders. But people forget that before she was famous, Twiggy was considered strange-looking and far from the norm. She was naturally thin, and despite the fact that the beauty ideals of the time taught her that her body shape wasn't attractive, she persevered and proved everyone wrong. And as she did so, she paved the path for unusual beauty. Because of her popularity, looking and dressing like a boy became just the sort of thing every girl wanted to do.

In the post-Twiggy era, androgyny subverts the idea of gender even further. There are women who work as models of male fashion (such as Casey Legler and Elliot Sailors), and men who model womenswear. The most famous of these was Andrej Pejić, an ethereal blonde who, after several years walking in both men's and women's runway shows, came out as transgender and transitioned to become a female model—she's now called Andreja Pejić. It goes to show, of course, that beauty takes all forms—and that clothing can go a long way toward helping you define who you are, whether that's a girl, a boy, or someone who'd rather not be labeled.

Long and lean Twiggy broke ground for androgynous fashion in the late 1960s.

Diana Vreeland

FASHION

Instigator

FULL NAME:
Diana Vreeland (née Dalziel)

BORN:
July 29, 1903, Paris, France

OCCUPATION:
Magazine editor, fashion journalist

BAD GIRL CRED:
Fashion editor supreme, Vreeland jolted the industry with her intrinsic style and theatricality, influencing how the world saw clothes.

A group of women sit in a New York restaurant in 1936. They're there for lunch, and in front of them on the table are small sandwiches, glasses of white wine, and a magazine, Harper's Bazaar. The magazine is open before them, and the women circle around it. "Why don't you ... Wear fruit hats? Currants? Cherries?" one reads aloud; the others titter. Another leans in and reads, "Why don't you ... Rinse your blond child's hair in dead champagne to keep it gold, as they do in France?" And then another reads in a somber tone, trying not to laugh: "Why don't you ... Have every room done up in every color green? This will take months, years, to collect, but it will be delightful—a melange of plants, green glass, green porcelains, and furniture covered in sad greens, gay greens, clear, faded and poison greens?" They scream with laughter, and all take a gulp of wine. "Who is the woman offering this outrageous advice?" one asks. Another leans in over the magazine: "It says her name is Diana Vreeland."

Diana Vreeland's flights of fancy weren't merely amusing: if it weren't for her influence, magazines wouldn't be what they are today. Widely regarded as one of the best fashion editors of all time, Vreeland shook up the printed page with her iconoclastic style and chaotically creative vision.

PART OF THE
Social whirl

Diana Vreeland's life was always unconventional. She was born in Paris to well-to-do parents, and her education mostly consisted of socializing with Paris's creative crème de la crème. (She was homeschooled, in an extremely informal way, and simply soaked up the social atmosphere provided by her well-connected family.) As a child she was particularly impressed by meeting Sergei Diaghilev, the founder of the Ballets Russes—a troupe whose influence on modern fashion has been far-reaching. When World War I broke out in 1914, Vreeland's family emigrated to America, and Vreeland was briefly enrolled in

school—but she promptly dropped out to attend ballet school instead.

Vreeland had many advantages in her life, but she was never considered beautiful. She had a large nose and a handsome face that many considered interesting, though not conventionally pretty. Her own mother made this very clear to Vreeland, who said, "I was always her ugly little monster." About herself Vreeland said, "I was the most hideous thing in the world." Instead of hiding, though, she learned to flaunt her unusual appearance, cutting her hair short to show off her profile. She adopted outrageous clothes and interesting

makeup: she would paint her lips scarlet, polish her eyelids, and use heavy marks of rouge on her cheeks, ears, and forehead. She called it her Kabuki look, after the dramatic Japanese dance theater form that uses heavy makeup.

By 1922, Vreeland was making a big impression on the social scene, aided by her dancing skills. She knew how to dress well, she knew how to move confidently through a room, and people noticed. That year, *Vogue* magazine, which was at that point focused more on society than on fashion, ran a photo of Vreeland (then known by her maiden name, Dalziel) with a car. The caption

Left: Vreeland in the late 1930s.
Opposite: the Ballets Russes.
Previous page: Vreeland in her *Vogue*
office in 1965.

read: "Such motors as these accelerate the social whirl. Miss Diana Dalziel, one of the most attractive debutantes of the winter, is shown entering her Cadillac." At age eighteen, she married a handsome gentleman named Reed Vreeland, and the two entered into a life of genteel domesticity in Albany, New York, while Reed trained at a bank. They then went to England, continuing their life of luxury; they drove a Bugatti, employed a butler, and holidayed in Scotland. Vreeland owned a lingerie shop in Mayfair, where she sold Spanish-made frivolities; her most famous client was Wallis Simpson.

THE BALLETS RUSSES

Formed in 1909 in Paris— the world's capital of fashion and art at the time—the Ballets Russes were a traveling dance company helmed by a creative impresario named Sergei Diaghilev. Known for collaborating with cutting-edge artists, composers, and fashion designers— people like Pablo Picasso, Igor Stravinsky, and Coco Chanel—the troupe had a huge influence on the aesthetics of the time. Its avant-garde, sensational costumes and sets were known for their bright colors and provocative sexuality.

DRESSING *the Part*

By 1936, the Vreelands had moved back to New York. And despite their wealth, they had a hard time maintaining their lifestyle in the expensive city. "I was going through money like one goes through … a bottle of scotch, I suppose, if you're an alcoholic," Vreeland commented. But luck was on her side. After a night dancing at the St. Regis Hotel in a glamorous white lace Chanel dress, she caught the eye of the editor of *Harper's Bazaar*, Carmel Snow, who could see that the woman had style. She was offered a job the very next day. "But Mrs. Snow, except for my little lingerie shop in London, I've never worked … I'm never dressed until lunch," Vreeland protested. "But you seem to know a lot about clothes," said Snow. And so was born "Why Don't You?," Vreeland's lighthearted and pointedly ridiculous column for society ladies, offering advice for maintaining a stylish lifestyle. Her column was considered creative but indulgent: she was the rich, eccentric aunt presiding over America's society ladies.

To the sound of a drumroll, a woman marches into an office foyer, the doors swinging behind her. "Good morning, Miss Prescott," the secretaries say; she doesn't acknowledge them. She sweeps into her office and presses a button, and her editors rush in in a flurry of heels and skirts. "I simply cannot release this issue as it is," she admonishes them, holding a copy of a magazine. And then she sees a swatch of fabric: "Ah, here is our answer: pink! … I want the whole issue pink! I want the whole country pink! From now on, girls … think pink!" And then the music begins.

Funny Face, a movie released in 1957, was all about a fashion magazine, and the character of the editor—a tempestuous, creative diva—was inspired by Diana Vreeland. It's easy to see why, because Vreeland's magazine years were the stuff of legend.

After "Why Don't You?," Vreeland was promoted by *Harper's Bazaar* to fashion editor, working alongside Carmel Snow and Alexey Brodovitch; together, they were seen as three pieces of a creative puzzle. Vreeland brought all the spirit and all the verve. She had an instinctive eye for what was next in fashion, and would modify outfits to suit her needs: removing shoulder pads, changing seams, and doing whatever else was necessary to make something chic. Notoriously, she got a late start to her day—she would work from home in the mornings and then come into the office for her lunch, which consisted of a peanut butter and jelly sandwich and a glass of Scotch. But she worked hard, and her daring fashion spreads helped turn *Harper's Bazaar* into the leading fashion magazine of the time. Vreeland developed a reputation for own her look, too: dark hair swept back severely, sometimes topped with a turban; dark, Kabuki-style makeup; and T-strap shoes.

But when Carmel Snow stepped down, Vreeland suffered an injustice: she did not get promoted to editor. Resentful, she bided her time until a position opened up at *Bazaar*'s chief rival, *Vogue*, in 1962. And so she jumped

VOGUE MAGAZINE

Vogue has existed in some form since 1892, when it was launched as a weekly paper catering to New York's upper classes. It didn't really become a fashion magazine until 1909, when its new owner, a man named Condé Nast, realized that he could make a lot of money off of women, who didn't have many magazines dedicated to their needs. Over its history, the magazine has had a number of editors, but it was Diana Vreeland who really cemented *Vogue* as fashion's bible.

ship to become associate editor. Less than a year later, *Vogue*'s editor resigned, and Vreeland was ready to begin a new era: as editor-in-chief of one of America's foremost fashion magazines. She painted the walls of her office a brilliant red (to match the walls of her house) and took the helm.

Vreeland, confidently executing her fashion ideas for *Vogue*.

weren't "traditionally" beautiful (just like herself)—people like Veruschka and Anjelica Huston. At a time when beauty was defined by hourglass figures and pert noses, these models were all gangly limbs, oversized features, and Grecian noses. She took risks in other ways, too; she printed the first photos of Mick Jagger, the lead singer of The Rolling Stones; she ran Truman Capote's story of a murder investigation; she printed photos of Jackson Pollock's experimental art—all unusual subjects for a fashion magazine at the time. She was extremely exacting with her demands, and sent photographers on daring missions; she once commissioned photographer Irving Penn to go to Spain to find her "the Gypsy queen who bathes in milk and has the most beautiful skin in the world!" And she changed the way fashion was presented. Prior to her, fashion photography was just about capturing the clothes, but she incorporated exotic locales and travel stories that turned fashion into a sort of adventure.

But all of Vreeland's wild creativity and uninhibited travel was, unfortunately, expensive. And when a financial recession hit in the '70s, paired with the career-focused second wave of feminism, which favored power suits over impractical fashion, Vreeland was dismissed. (Her successor, Grace Mirabella, painted her office beige.)

Vreeland's time at *Vogue* coincided with the beginning of the Swinging Sixties, when the hippie movement brought edgy counterculture values into mainstream awareness. Vreeland pushed the magazine as far, creatively, as she could. She routinely featured models who had unusual features, who

FASHION SPOTLIGHT
Anna Wintour

FULL NAME:

Anna Wintour

BORN:

November 3, 1949, London, England

OCCUPATION:

Magazine editor, fashion journalist

BAD GIRL CRED:

**For years, Wintour has been the most feared
and respected person in fashion—for good reason.**

Even Anna Wintour's nicknames are enough to strike fear into the hearts of many: "Nuclear Wintour," "The Wintour of Our Discontent." With her helmetlike bob, sunglasses, and famously hard personality, the longtime *Vogue* editor is a force to be reckoned with, both inside the fashion world and out. She was the inspiration for the film *The Devil Wears Prada*, about a young woman who goes to work as the assistant to a tyrannical fashion editor in New York. The devil, of course, is Wintour.

Wintour wasn't always so scary. She was born into a journalistic London family; her father was the editor of the *Evening Standard*. She went to a posh private school, where she rebelled against the dress code by hemming her skirts short; she first cut her hair into a bob at age fourteen. She was interested in fashion, and buried herself in style magazines imported from America. At fifteen, she started working at hip fashion boutique Biba, which was known for being one of the first places to sell minidresses. At the same time, she became a regular on London's edgy nightclub scene, dating a series of older, influential men. By the following year she had dropped out of school to begin a training program at Harrods, a high-end department store. By 1970, at twenty-one, she had her first magazine job, as an editorial assistant at fashion magazine *Harper's & Queen*, where she produced inventive fashion spreads. But by 1975 she had moved to New York with her boyfriend, seeking greener fields.

That year, she took a job at *Harper's Bazaar*, but her shoots were too daring for management, who fired her after a few short months (she committed the crime of giving a model dreadlocks for a couture shoot). And then she got her first real job as a fashion editor—at *Viva*, a women's erotic magazine operated by the editor of the pornographic men's magazine *Penthouse*. There, she promoted the work of daring fashion photographers like Helmut Newton, and proved that she was willing to take risks. After that magazine shuttered, she worked a series of other magazine jobs until she found her way to *Vogue* in the 1980s. She took editorship of U.S. *Vogue* in 1988.

From the start at *Vogue*, Wintour was revolutionary. She changed the aesthetic of the magazine, moving it away from the previous editor's lifestyle focus to refocus on fashion. She also mixed high and low fashion, pairing expensive designer items with cheaper, mass-market clothes in a way that hadn't been seen before. She was notoriously hard to please and tough on her staff—hence the nicknames. But she has become, without dispute, the most influential person in fashion. Designers vet their collections with her, and if she doesn't like something, it's the kiss of death. She advises fashion houses on who to hire, and has made the careers of many young designers. The *Guardian* newspaper named her the "unofficial mayoress" of New York for the power she wields. But the key to Wintour's success is her iron-clad self-confidence and willingness to take risks. She may be the mayoress, but it was a job she seized, not one she was elected to.

Wintour posing at a 2012 gala, complete with her signature bob.

NEVER
Out of Style

It's 1973, and a crowd is walking through a gallery. In the center of the gallery are mannequins dressed in beautiful couture fashions. The light hits the mannequins in a dramatic way—a face gazes into the light, an arm falls into shadow. Arms and legs are posed in such a way that they look like they were caught in motion. "It's like they're dancing," sighs one of the onlookers. "Dancing in Balenciaga."

Vreeland styling model Marisa Berenson.

After her dismissal from *Vogue*, Vreeland didn't make a scene. Instead, she vanished for four months, immersing herself in travel. But upon her return, she received an interesting proposition: to take over the reins of the Costume Institute at the Metropolitan Museum of Art in New York.

At the time, the Costume Institute was not a popular destination for the public. It was really just a reference for fashion historians—but Vreeland, of course, saw that in a new light, it could look dramatically different. She began to stage ambitious exhibitions. The first was "The World of Balenciaga"; others that followed included "The Glory of Russian Costume," "Diaghilev: Costumes and Designs of the Ballets Russes," and "The Eighteenth-Century Woman." Vreeland approached her shows with an eye for drama, playing with lighting and posing the mannequins so that they looked like the sort of people who might have actually worn the clothes in the past. Sometimes she did things that truly challenged convention; for example, when she disliked how old some vintage shirts from the couture label Mainbocher looked, she demanded to have replicas made, so that they would look as they would have when new. If she couldn't find the original of a certain fashion piece she wanted to include, she would commission a designer to make a replica. For a history museum, devoted to preserving the past, this was radical—but Vreeland's allegiance was to the spirit of fashion, not to the fact of it. And the public responded to her theatricality: just as she had done for the pages of *Vogue*, she had made the once-stuffy fashion exhibitions at the Met fun. Her shows drew crowds in the millions, and the Institute had to keep her exhibitions open for months to accommodate the demand.

When Vreeland passed away in 1989, her memorial service was held at the Met. Though she was once quoted as saying "I loathe nostalgia," four hundred of her famous friends from fashionable society came out to pay their regards. And in 1993, she was honored in an exhibition of her own at the Met: "Diana Vreeland: Immoderate Style." Her reputation still looms large over magazines today. As her colleague Richard Avedon said at the time of her death, "She was and remains the only genius fashion editor."

ICONIC LOOK № 6

GRACE CODDINGTON

When she was young, **GRACE CODDINGTON** was a model; when she grew older, she became a fashion editor for *Vogue*. Her wit and resolve are inspirational for fashion followers, especially after her star turn in the 2009 film *The September Issue*, a documentary about the making of *Vogue*. And her look is distinctly her own: minimal makeup, pale skin, and black clothing—all taking side stage to her long, poofy, bright orange hair.

FASHION SPOTLIGHT
Tavi Gevinson

FULL NAME:

Tavi Gevinson

BORN:

April 21, 1996, Chicago, Illinois

OCCUPATION:

Blogger, magazine editor

BAD GIRL CRED:

Gevinson has given a voice to teenage girls through her self-made media empire.

Tavi Gevinson's life began in a suburb of Chicago called Oak Park, where she grew up in a middle-class neighborhood with an English-teacher dad and a textile-artist mom. In many ways it was an average upbringing, but Gevinson was a precocious child. At age eleven, in 2008, she began a blog. It was called *Style Rookie*, and featured surprisingly adult musings on fashion interspersed with photos of Gevinson modeling her own imaginative ensembles.

Gevinson's appearance was unusual for a girl her age: she dyed her hair a bluish gray, wore granny glasses, and mixed patterns and styles with the verve and creativity of a full-grown fashion editor. And it got her noticed. Soon, *Style Rookie* was a runaway success. She caught the attention of fashion editors and the public, and was adopted by the fashion community as a kind of curiosity. The editors at British magazine *Pop* put Gevinson on the magazine's cover in 2009, and she managed to score some writing gigs, too, most notably a column in *Harper's Bazaar*. She was invited to Fashion Week, and she befriended *Vogue* editor Anna Wintour. By thirteen, Gevinson was a bona fide fashion celebrity with impressive clout.

At the time, though, a lot of people didn't take her very seriously—simply because she was so young. Gevinson was achieving things at age thirteen that had taken others well into their adult years to manage, and people were bitter. One writer, Lesley M.M. Blume, called her a "novelty." But that didn't turn out to be the case. Reflecting on the backlash, Gevinson later said, "A lot of people on the Internet have a problem with a young person doing well. I felt like, there were people who were [at Fashion Week] because of their name, their money or their family, and I didn't have any of those things."

In 2011, at the ripe old age of fifteen, Gevinson decided to change direction. She thought it was time to focus less on fashion and more on feminism. And so with the help of Jane Pratt (a seasoned magazine editor known for hip '90s teen magazine *Sassy*), she started an online magazine called *Rookie*. With *Rookie*, Gevinson aimed to encourage independent thought and creativity among teenage girls, fostering a tight-knit community of people like her. Featuring writing and illustration from a wide variety of contributors, most of whom were teenagers themselves, *Rookie* took off quickly, and readers (some of whom were adults) flocked to its quirky DIY aesthetic. It was a space where teenage girls could finally be themselves: experiment with style;

embrace their body type, ethnicity, and sexual identity; and learn how to assert their opinions. The media praised Gevinson for the way she managed to smartly combine pop culture, fashion, and feminism. And as *Rookie* matured, Gevinson did too; she abandoned the eclectic grandma styles of her earlier teenage years in favor of a retro, 1950s, pared-down look that she modeled after the sweater-clad teenagers of '90s cult TV show *Twin Peaks*.

As Gevinson racks up the accolades (she has twice appeared on the *Forbes* 30 Under 30 in Media list, and was named one of the 25 Most Influential Teens of 2014 by *Time*) she continues to try new things. She's appeared as an actress in films and off-Broadway plays. Regardless of where she's going, she remains a beacon for teenage girls, leading them down a path that's weird, creative, and self-chosen.

Gevinson in 2015, showing off her eclectic sense of style.

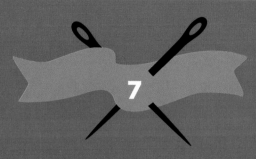

Madonna

FASHION

Chameleon

FULL NAME:
Madonna Louise Ciccone

BORN:
August 16, 1958, Bay City, Michigan

OCCUPATION:
Musician, actress, businesswoman

BAD GIRL CRED:
A chameleon of style and champion of women's power,
Madonna has never stopped expressing herself and
shocking the public with what she wears—or doesn't.

On a canal boat in Venice, a woman wearing a black crop top leans back provocatively, her midriff bared above a chunky metallic belt buckle; she's dancing. Her neck is loaded with layers of string bead necklaces, and her hair is curly, blonde, and cropped to her chin. On her ears, she wears enormous, glittery stars, and her lips are a dark cherry. As she daringly meets the viewer's eyes, she's singing: "Like a virgin ... Touched for the very first time! Like a virgin, when your heart beats, next to mine."

Madonna: she's known as the Queen of Pop, the Material Girl, and Madge. She's widely acknowledged as the most powerful and influential woman in music in the late twentieth and early twenty-first centuries. But at the mention of her name, the first thing that will come to mind for many people isn't a song but an image. A blonde girl in a crop top, a woman in a cone bra, a dominatrix boxing into the camera: they're all boundary-pushing characters Madonna Ciccone took on, using fashion to make a point—and make her name.

GIRL
on the Make

Madonna grew up in a large, mostly Italian-American Catholic family. Her mother died when Madonna was six years old; her father married the family housekeeper and had even more children. Madonna's new stepmother was strict, and young Madonna rebelled against her tough rules, but at school she was always at the top of her game, getting straight A's. In high school she wasn't a popular kid, and with her interests in music and ballet, she got branded as an arty weirdo. She decided to play up her outsider image, and refused to shave her legs or wear makeup, not wanting to conform to the girly-girl ideal. After high school, she spent a year at the University of Michigan studying dance, then finally made her escape: with only $35 to her name, she moved to New York to work as a dancer.

It was tough for Madonna in New York at first. She did get work as a backup dancer, but she had to also work as a waitress in a doughnut shop in order to make ends meet. Eventually her dancing gig led her to a relationship with a musician, with whom she formed a band called The Breakfast Club. From that band, she moved on to another band, Emmy, before she rebranded herself. She first signed as a solo act with a record label in 1982, boldly using only her first name, Madonna.

Madonna's first two singles were playful, dance-friendly club hits; her third single, "Holiday," was a global chart-topper. And immediately, Madonna's appearance struck a chord with people. Her look borrowed from punk and street fashion, and she wore her hair short, bleached blonde, and falling into her face like a pompadour. She favored crop tops and sneakers, skirts worn over leggings, fishnets, and stacks of bracelets that snaked up her arms. Her favorite symbol was a crucifix, which she wore irreverently,

on earrings and necklaces. (She developed the look in collaboration with a jewelry designer named Maripol, who was eager to sell her wares.) Madonna's style caught on fast, and soon teenage girls around the world were parroting her insolent mall-chic.

MADONNA'S MOVIES

Madonna is mostly known for her music, but she has also had an on-again, off-again career as an actress, having starred in more than twenty feature films. The first of these was *Desperately Seeking Susan* (1985). While her acting wasn't praised, her wardrobe for the film—classic early Madonna, with funky jewelry, off-the-shoulder T-shirts, and big hair—was extremely influential.

ICONIC LOOK № 7

FLAT TOP

SQUARE SHOULDERS

MEN'S ARMANI JACKET

GRACE JONES

GRACE JONES was the androgynous, shape-shifting disco queen of the 1970s and '80s. Born in Barbados in 1948, she moved with her family to New York when she was a teenager, and became a highly successful model, particularly in Paris, a city that celebrated her unusual looks. In the '70s, she transitioned to a career in music, and her edgy, fashion-forward, gender-bending look became one of the iconic images of the era. She was known for her futuristic cool, her flat-top haircut, her avant-garde menswear, and her lanky, mannish frame.

SINNER or SAINT

Madonna, however, was not content with maintaining the status quo. Throughout her career, she has been known as a master of reinvention, changing her sound and her image with each album. For her second album, *Like a Virgin*, she toyed with the concept of her name (in classical Italian art, the name Madonna is often used to refer to Mary, the virgin mother of Jesus), and played it off her newly sultry image by posing provocatively in a wedding dress. Conservative and religious groups condemned Madonna, but she inspired young women, who loved her open embrace of her sexuality and her brazen confidence. That album also contained the single "Material Girl," which earned Madonna both a lifelong nickname and comparisons to Marilyn Monroe, who she mimicked in the music video. By her fourth album, *Like a Prayer* (which she dedicated to her mother), she was grappling further with her understanding of religion and male/female power dynamics.

Her music video for the title track was extremely controversial: it features a busty Madonna who reversed traditional gender roles by taking a dominant, aggressive role as the romantic pursuer; in the end, she makes out with a black actor dressed as a saint. It earned her an official reprimand from the Vatican.

The furor over Madonna's image didn't stop there. In 1990 she caused another scandal, on her Blond Ambition tour. Christian groups opposed the way she juxtaposed religious imagery with sexuality, while the provocative outfits for the tour, designed by Jean Paul Gaultier, became the stuff of legend. In particular, the "cone bra," a metallic-pink bodysuit with a brassiere sporting two pointy cones for cups, became both infamous and iconic. You can see its echoes in the campy, amped-up sexuality of younger performers like Katy Perry, with her cupcake bra in her video for "California Gurls."

Madonna, playing with religious imagery on a magazine cover in 1987.

MADONNA

Madonna performing in her cone bra in 1990.

Though today it's common to see pop stars performing in stylized lingerie, Madonna was one of the first to use underwear as outerwear.

That same year, something happened that pushed Madonna toward another transformation. The edgy, sexually suggestive black-and-white video for her song "Justify My Love" was banned from television for being too explicit—which made Madonna decide that exploring her sexuality was *just* the thing to do.

JUSTIFY MY RATING

In movies, TV, and music videos, bans and R-ratings are often due to sexual content, not violence— even if the sexual content is loving and consensual. Recognizing that hypocrisy, Madonna quipped: "Why is it that people are willing to go to a movie and watch someone get blown to bits for no reason and nobody wants to see two girls kissing or two men snuggling?"

FASHION SPOTLIGHT
Marilyn Monroe

FULL NAME:
Norma Jeane Mortenson

BORN:
June 1, 1926, Los Angeles, California

OCCUPATION:
Actress

BAD GIRL CRED:
**Monroe carefully crafted her image
to seduce the world.**

A blonde woman standing over a New York City subway grate, the wind from the tunnel below billowing the skirt of her white dress around her legs as she clutches it and laughs: it's one of the most iconic images of the twentieth century, and proof of Marilyn Monroe's status as the ultimate sex symbol. It's also a prime example of the carefully crafted image Monroe created for herself.

Glamour wasn't a part of Monroe's childhood. Born with the rather plain name of Norma Jeane Mortenson, she spent her childhood in foster homes because her mother was unable to care for her. But when she was nineteen years old and working in a factory during World War II, she was spotted by a photographer, there to take morale-boosting photos for a patriotic magazine. Those shots led Monroe to a successful career in modeling, and soon after that, she was on movie screens across America and around the world in big-budget films like *Gentlemen Prefer Blondes* and *The Seven Year Itch*.

In movies and public appearances, Marilyn was the mid-twentieth century's dream of a seductress. She was a blonde vixen with an hourglass figure, a total sex symbol. But just as she played characters in movies, she was acting out the role of a sex symbol in her own life. She crafted her image very carefully: to emphasize her generous curves, she wore dresses so tight that seamstresses had to sew her into them (supposedly, she told them to do so in such a way as to outline the curves of each individual buttock), and taking a tip from the burlesque dancers of the day, she didn't wear underwear (to avoid pesky lines). A stickler for detail, she had a cobbler make one of her heels ever so slightly shorter than the other, causing her to swing her hips even more as she walked. She touched up her dyed-blonde hair every five days, and when she put on lipstick, she wore five different shades of red, outlining her lips and filling in the shadows to form a perfect, glossy pout.

Unfortunately, Marilyn was deeply unhappy, and fame didn't help; she committed suicide when she was thirty-six, still very much an icon. But her mark on our culture was so strong that images of her pop up everywhere more than fifty years after her death. Her way of dressing, too, is still imitated. And when people style themselves like Marilyn, it's more than just fashion. Her image is laden with meaning, something her most famous imitator, Madonna, definitely knew when she openly copied her look in her video for

"Material Girl," subverting Marilyn's vulnerability and replacing it with cocky self-assuredness. Others have taken a more literal approach; Lindsay Lohan, an actress whose career has suffered due to her own erratic behavior, posed as her in *New York* magazine in 2008, channeling Marilyn's more troubled side. And yet the aim of both imitators is similar. No matter who's wearing that figure-hugging dress and those blonde curls, they're making a claim to sexual power.

This famous photo from 1954 shows Monroe flirtatiously posing over a subway grate while filming *The Seven Year Itch.*

ARTIST *Provocateur*

A couple of twelve-year-old girls run into the bookstore, giggling excitedly. "Where is it?" one says to the other. "I don't know," the other replies, and they walk up to the counter. "Uh ...," the first girl stutters, looking up at the clerk. "Do you have Madonna's book here?" The clerk, a middle-aged woman, laughs gently. "We do, and it's certainly interesting," she says with a wink, "but you guys are much too young to buy it." She points behind her, where a large, metallic-covered book sits on a shelf, emblazoned with the word SEX. "We keep it behind the counter, but you're welcome to come back and buy it when you're eighteen." Dejected, the two girls turn and head for the door.

By 1992, Madonna was pushing hard for more control of her career and her image. After starring in a feminist movie about an all-girl baseball team, *A League of Their Own*, she started her own entertainment company, Maverick, which produced a wide range of media: films, music, television, books, and more. Importantly, Maverick allowed Madonna the creative freedom to do whatever she wanted without having to please company executives—a bold move in the world of pop music, where performers, especially females, often have their images and career moves tightly managed. And the first project that Madonna pursued with Maverick shocked both her fans and society: a photographic coffee table book called *SEX*, featuring arty photos of Madonna and other people in various states of undress. Rather than challenging people with her clothing, this time Madonna was challenging people with her utter lack of it. The book, initially, wasn't very well received. A few countries tried to

Madonna performing in subversive dominatrix-inspired fashion during her Girlie Show tour in 1993.

ban it, while many bookstores in the United States kept it behind the counter due to its explicit nature. Some people may not have liked it, but with this book, Madonna established herself as a champion for female sexuality. She said, at the time, "I don't think sex is bad. I don't think nudity is bad. I don't think that being in touch with your sexuality and being able to talk about it is bad."

The release of *SEX* coincided with the release of Madonna's first album on Maverick, *Erotica*. The album explored similar themes of sexuality, and on the tour for the album, The Girlie Show, Madonna played with transgressive images, dressing up as everything from a dominatrix to Marlene Dietrich. All the costumes were created by Dolce & Gabbana, who were known for their sexy designs.

In 1996, Madonna began filming the movie *Evita*. She played the title character, Eva Perón, the one-time First Lady of Argentina, a woman who, Madonna commented, people saw as either "a saint or the incarnation of Satan"—clearly something she could relate to. After the film wrapped, Madonna gave birth to her first child; over the next few years, she had a second, and adopted two more.

THE Virgin Mother

Becoming a mother made Madonna think more deeply about her relationship to the world. She began to experiment with yoga, and studied both Hinduism and Kabbalah (a mystical school of thought within Judaism). The new spirituality crept into both her look and her sound. Her next album, *Ray of Light*, was a buoyant experiment in electronica that incorporated Eastern-influenced melodies, and a newly centered Madonna appeared in public wearing a sari, a bindi, and mehndi painted on her hands, all of which carry religious and cultural symbolism for South Asian people. Some people suggested that this was an act of cultural appropriation—that is, that Madonna stole from another culture without really respecting it. Regardless, her new appearance and sound inspired millions of Western women to take an interest in Eastern culture and fashion.

SOUTH ASIAN FASHION

Saris, bindis, and mehndi are all traditional elements of South Asian women's fashion, worn in such countries as India, Pakistan, Sri Lanka, Nepal, and Bangladesh. A sari is a wrap dress that can be styled in many ways: one of the most popular styles is draped over the shoulder and hip, leaving the midriff bare. A bindi is a decoration placed in the middle of the forehead to symbolize wisdom. Mehndi is a henna paste applied in complex, swirling designs to women's hands or feet for festive occasions.

South Asian women often apply mehndi for weddings and religious holidays.

When women become mothers and enter middle age, they face the expectation that they will be well behaved, and certainly not sexual. As Madonna got older, however, she continued to push back against what she was *supposed* to be, and also refused to accept that she could be only one thing. In 2003, at age forty-five, she wrote her first book: an illustrated story for children called *The English Roses*. At the book launch, she presented herself as a

prim and proper English lady, resplendent in a formfitting white, floral-patterned, tea-length dress. But a mere month earlier, she had gotten onstage at the MTV Video Music Awards to perform a version of "Like a Virgin" alongside then-reigning pop starlets Britney Spears and Christina Aguilera; the two younger women wore white, while Madonna, in a sexy black bodysuit, kissed them passionately on their respective mouths. She didn't tone it down after that: in 2014, the fifty-six-year-old posed for *Interview* magazine in a racy, fashion-forward spread. Completely unwilling to give in to her critics, Madonna made it clear that women of all ages could be sexual beings—and mothers and successful businesswomen, and often all three at once.

Madonna's influence on style is indisputable, but even more important is her influence on culture. She wears what she wants to, and often to prove a point: that she doesn't have boundaries, and that she can do whatever she wants. It's a lesson that many women of her generation and later generations have taken to heart, whether they're on the dance floor or on the job.

Madonna at fifty-four, proving she can wear whatever she wants, wherever she wants.

FASHION SPOTLIGHT
Rihanna

FULL NAME:

Robyn Rihanna Fenty

BORN:

February 20, 1988, Saint Michael, Barbados

OCCUPATION:

Musician

BAD GIRL CRED:

With her daring fashion sense, Rihanna will never cave to her haters.

"**Customers don't care** any more about reviews or hard-copy publications," designer Tom Ford told Style. com in 2014. "They care what picture Rihanna just Instagrammed while she's naked in bed, what new shoes she has on, how she's talking about them. That's what they respond to." And perhaps it shouldn't come as a surprise that the photos taken by the Barbadian pop star are more influential on fashion than any review: after all, Rihanna has proven that she's a true fashion innovator, and willing to take risks—without caring what you think about it, either.

At first, life wasn't easy for Rihanna. Her dad was a drug addict who scored crack on street corners, and due to family turmoil, her parents ended up divorcing. Her mom, who worked as an accountant, had to spend very long hours at the office to make enough money to support the family. Fourteen-year-old Rihanna played mom, taking care of her two little brothers. And while her mother wanted her to dress like a proper young woman, self-sufficient Rihanna started doing her own thing; she hung around with the boys, and she dressed like them, too, wearing ball caps, jeans, and T-shirts. Meanwhile, at school, she formed a girl group with two of her friends. And

then, one day, like magic, life changed. When Rihanna was fifteen, her singing group managed to get an audition with a major producer, who was riveted by Rihanna's commanding presence and killer voice. In 2005, when Rihanna was seventeen, she had an audition for the label Def Jam, which was headed by Jay Z. She ended up signing a six-album deal.

When Rihanna's first album came out, her public image was not very daring—baggy jeans, midriff-baring tops, and sweet dresses. But by the time her third one, *Good Girl Gone Bad*, rolled around, things had changed ... dramatically. Gone were the curls and jean skirts that had dominated her tentative early wardrobe; now Rihanna had an edgy, angular haircut and sexier, more fashion-forward clothing. She began to take risks; she became known for not wearing a bra (unladylike!) and defiantly embracing her sexuality—posing in provocative photos, making no secret of the fact that she was a fan of partying and hooking up, and generally not caring if people gossiped or called her a slut. At the same time, she kept riffing on menswear themes, in deference to her tomboy past: she wore oversized men's jackets over everything. As her wardrobe grew more daringly eclectic, she became known for dramatic transformations, claiming Madonna's chameleonic career as inspiration. In one of her most headline-stealing fashion moments, she wore a completely sheer silver gown with a matching headwrap to the 2014 CFDA Fashion Awards—a daring nod to Josephine Baker.

Rihanna's music may have topped the charts, but she also became famous for using fashion as a tool to define her iconoclastic image and speak to her ardent fans. Instagram helped her do that, and she became one of its savviest users. On her account on the social photosharing app (@badgalriri), she posted her ensembles and her exploits, replete with both partying and fashion. By 2014, she had over 14 million followers, and her account was sparking trends: designers from Balmain to Tom Ford issued collections that looked suspiciously like something Riri would wear. She secured endorsement deals and ad campaigns, and won a CFDA Icon award. And she's still so young— Rihanna's influence has years to grow.

Rihanna in 2011, dressed in outrageous style.

Rei Kawakubo

anti FASHION

FULL NAME:
Rei Kawakubo

BORN:
October 11, 1942, Tokyo, Japan

OCCUPATION:
Fashion designer

BAD GIRL CRED:
Ragged, tattered, lumpy, boxy: Kawakubo made
ugly interesting, and changed the meaning of
fashion for women who refuse to fit the mold.

The crowd sits silently as the women stalk toward them in dark flocks, their clothing ragged shrouds of black. The lights flash ominously and the only sound is the beat of a drum. The clothes are misshapen and strange: skirts with sleeves stitched to the front of them, sweaters with neck holes cut into the shoulder or chest, and huge overcoats buttoned from the left to the right. The effect is almost frightening. The models wear makeup that makes them look old, tired, and sometimes scarred, and they soldier along grimly in their dark, asymmetrical attire. One fashion journalist shakes her head. "It's apocalyptic!" she exclaims. Another looks amazed. "It's revolutionary!"

Before Rei Kawakubo, fashion was usually beautiful—sometimes controversial, but still recognizable as clothing. The Japanese fashion designer, whose aesthetic was often referred to as "apocalyptic," changed all that. In the 1980s, her radical refusal of traditional female beauty rocked the fashion world to its core.

THE CALM
Before the Storm

Anarchic, tattered, deconstructed anti-fashion may be what Rei Kawakubo is known for, but the influential fashion designer's childhood was anything but dark. Her family was fairly well-off: her dad was an administrator at a respected Tokyo university, while her mother, who had studied to be an English teacher, stayed at home with Rei and her two siblings and made clothes for the family. When the kids got old enough, Kawakubo's mother wanted to go back to work—and Kawakubo's father forbade her from doing so. (In Japan at the time, men were in charge of the household.) But Kawakubo's mother

defied his command, left him, and got a job. And so Kawakubo's strong-willed single mother gave her a role model for real independence.

Kawakubo ended up going to the university where her father worked, and she studied the history of aesthetics. But after university, she decided to go her own way. Without saying a word to her parents, she moved to Tokyo's most bohemian neighborhood, Harajuku. There she soaked up the rebellious attitude and unusual fashion in the streets surrounding her shared apartment. At the time, Tokyo wasn't a hub for the fashion industry—but Kawakubo didn't have plans to work in fashion. When it came down to finding a job, she ended up working at a textile manufacturer. Her position was in the advertising department, where she found an outlet for her creativity searching for props and costumes for the ads. She enjoyed collaborating with photographers and art directors on these projects, and after three years,

Opposite: The wild fashion of Harajuku. Page 145: Kawakubo's aesthetic is often anarchic; this display she created for Comme des Garçons in 2007 is a good example.

HARAJUKU FASHION

Harajuku street style is world famous. People dress up to show off in styles like Gothic Lolita (dark, Edwardian, doll-like clothing), Visual Kei (glam rock), and Mori Girl (loose, layered, forest-princess clothing in greens and browns).

she went freelance as a stylist. Now on her own, she had even more creative leeway—when she was unable to find the right item of clothing for a project, she'd design it herself. In this way, Kawakubo became a self-taught clothing designer whose methods were all her own.

Kawakubo's success as a stylist allowed her to pursue clothing design more seriously. By 1969, she was renting her own studio and employing assistants, and edgy Tokyo shops catering to young people stocked her designs. She called her label Comme des Garçons, which means "Like Boys" in French. She claimed to be making clothes for someone "who is not swayed by what her husband thinks." Many have speculated that the name Comme des Garçons is meant to suggest the antifeminine nature of her clothing, which at the time resembled the loose and practical clothing worn by fishermen. But Kawakubo has maintained throughout the years that she just liked the way it sounds. By 1973 Kawakubo had opened her first boutique; her brand

became increasingly popular in Japan, and by 1980 she had 150 stores in the country. Within Japan, followers of her brand, which featured a lot of dark, draping silhouettes, were called "the crows."

DEVOTEES OF COMME DES GARÇONS

Comme des Garçons tends to attract fans who are known for being a little weird.
A few people who like to wear the brand:

BJÖRK

Icelandic musician known for wearing strange clothing and producing experimental music.

TILDA SWINTON

British actress famous for taking daring roles in independent and mainstream films.

CHLOË SEVIGNY

American actress and sometime fashion designer known equally for her acting and her outré fashion choices.

JOHN WATERS

Cult film director whose movies celebrate "trash" culture and social outcasts.

FASHION SPOTLIGHT
Cindy Sherman

FULL NAME:
Cynthia Morris Sherman

BORN:
January 19, 1954, Glen Ridge, New Jersey

OCCUPATION:
Photographer

BAD GIRL CRED:
**Sherman uses photography to question
our ideals of beauty.**

Clothing has the power to transform our identity, and also to shape it, twist it, and hide it: it's a concept that the work of American photographer Cindy Sherman explores and exploits, to great acclaim.

Sherman, an immensely successful American artist, is known for her self-portraits, in which she takes on a different persona using elaborate costuming and makeup. Her photos are often confrontational: she uses clothing to challenge both the roles women take in society and the way women are portrayed in the media.

She got her start at Buffalo State College, where she rebelled against the perceived conservatism of painting by taking up photography. One of the people she met there, an artist named Robert Longo, encouraged her to document her process of "dolling up" to go out to parties, an idea that may have contributed to her elaborate lifelong game of dress-up.

Sherman's first big show, "Untitled Film Stills," was a set of sixty-nine photographs in which Sherman dressed up as clichéd characters from the films of the 1950s and '60s. She appears as a series of women—bombshells, housewives, career girls—all portrayed through different clothing, makeup, and poses. Viewed together, the photographs show how we often see the world through stereotypes and clichés. Throughout her career, Sherman has played with these ideas, often to devastating effect. She has dressed up as centerfolds from erotic men's magazines, showing the unhappiness of the characters; played up the hopes and dreams of washed-up actresses, using Hollywood-style headshots; and parodied the quest for eternal youth and perfection among society women.

Many of Sherman's images show-case people who are "ugly" or who typify ugly things in society. For this reason, she has had some interesting collaborations with the fashion world—which has frequently inspired both her work and her critiques. For example, in 1983 she created fashion shoots for two different brands: one for *Interview* magazine, and another for French *Vogue*. The shoots share a strong anti-fashion stance: the model, Sherman herself, looks dejected, confused, and unhappy, and poses awkwardly in her clothing. In 1994, she collaborated with Rei Kawakubo on a series of postcard advertisements for Comme des Garçons. Sherman applied herself eagerly to Kawakubo's strange aesthetic, and the images show a grouchy, defiantly unpretty Sherman posing in odd scenes, breaking the rules of fashion photography by making the clothing less important than the character she is creating. She took this approach to even greater extremes for a 2008 campaign for the French design house Balenciaga. In that series, "fashion victims" like magazine editors, fashion buyers, and publicity hacks (all played by Sherman) pose in often grotesque ways that don't look at all glamorous, all while wearing Balenciaga clothing. (It may not have been pretty, but it certainly lent Balenciaga a little art-world cool.)

In her work, Sherman strikes a delicate balance: she's reliant on clothing to tell her story, and yet highly critical of fashion's commercial image and the darker side of how we use clothing to shape our own images. She's an artist, but a commercial one too, and for fashion-savvy viewers, her work is a lesson in how fashion shapes the way we see each other.

Typically "ugly" self-portraits of Sherman playing different characters.

For the
BIRDS

A model in Yohji Yamamoto's designs in 2010.

In the '70s and '80s, Kawakubo was romantically involved with another young designer, Yohji Yamamoto. Yamamoto shared her creative ethos and penchant for dark, destroyed clothing, and the two competed with each other and thrived off each other's energy. And in 1981 they shared a huge landmark: they debuted their collections internationally, at Paris Fashion Week. The press took notice of the two avant-garde collections, but the designers didn't truly shake up the fashion world until the following year, when they showed their Spring/Summer 1983 collections. The fashions were aggressive, misshapen, and disturbing, in a palette of dark colors. Some called Kawakubo's collection "post-atomic"—as in, what people might wear after a nuclear bomb hit. But most recognized it as a radical departure for women's clothing. Kawakubo, along with Yamamoto, had created a new aesthetic, and one that was not pretty, or feminine, or traditional in any way. Instead, her clothing was challenging, artistic, and interesting.

"Quasimodo!" the photographer yells into the silent room. A couple of people in the crowd stifle laughter. In front of them, a line of models walk down a runway. The one the photographer is yelling at has a large bump above her shoulders; she looks like a hunchback. But the other girls all look strange, too. They wear clingy dresses in bright gingham patterns, but beneath the pretty silhouettes, strange shapes lurk. One girl has a misshapen lump above her bottom; another has an oddly protruding belly that makes her look almost pregnant. But it's not the girls who are misshapen—it's the dresses.

By the 1990s, Kawakubo was extremely successful internationally, and had become renowned for her distressed, ragged minimalism. While she was never going to be a mainstream favorite, her designs were coveted by a certain kind of fashion obsessive. In that decade, too, she and her lover Yohji Yamamoto, who had shared so much in terms of creative direction, split up—and in 1992 Kawakubo married Adrian Joffe, an executive in her company. This emotional time, though painful, offered inspiration for Kawakubo's designs. Her next collection was titled "The Broken Bride," and it borrowed from the myth of Lilith (see page 154). The dresses were flowing and had chiffon veils, all in a deep purple.

Though Kawakubo's early collections showed her anarchic creativity, she continued to up the ante even after she was established as a major designer.

LILITH

In Jewish mythology, Lilith (depicted here in an 1868 painting) is a symbol of wanton feminine power. According to the story, God creates Lilith at the same time as Adam, and she becomes his first wife. But Lilith is not the passive sort: she's also a kind of demon, who can fly, enjoys sex, and has destructive tendencies. Most important, she doesn't put up with being treated badly: because Adam doesn't treat her as his equal, she leaves him. She flees to the Red Sea, and refuses to reconcile with him. Because of her defiant attitude, modern feminists have adopted her as a symbol of feminine power.

In 1995, Kawakubo challenged the boundaries of taste and created a storm of controversy when she showed a collection that resembled the pajama-like outfits of prisoners in Nazi concentration camps. (She publicly apologized for offending people.) But her most infamous collection was "Dress Meets Body, Body Meets Dress" from 1997. The inspiration for the collection? Kawakubo was angered by a display at the Gap clothing chain that featured humdrum monochromatic clothes—which she saw as ripping off her own color palette in an extremely boring way. "Dress Meets Body, Body Meets Dress" was the polar opposite. The dresses in the collection were pretty, and clung to the body—except that they featured large, strategically placed lumps inside them that made the wearer look disfigured. Journalists nicknamed it the "lumps and bumps collection." Critics were puzzled, and eventually Kawakubo relented by making the lumps removable, so that more people might wear the dresses.

BAG ISM

YOKO ONO

ICONIC LOOK № 8

An avant-garde artist and musician active since the 1950s, **YOKO ONO** has always had a distinctive style. She favors dark colors and sleek contours, and wears her long, dark hair parted in the middle. Her classic look is pared-down artistic chic. But as an artist, she sometimes makes more aggressive statements with her clothing. One famous example comes from the late 1960s, when she (together with her husband, John Lennon of The Beatles) advocated that people wear bags. She called this movement "bagism," the idea being that wearing a bag allowed you to avoid the prejudices that come from being visible. Age, gender, race, or style simply don't come into play when you're wearing a bag.

INDEPENDENT *woman*

Season after season, Kawakubo has proven herself a master of reinvention. For her, success has very little to do with whether she is liked. In fact, when her designs are received too warmly, she considers it a failure. "I do not feel happy when a collection is understood too well," she says. Despite, or perhaps because of, Kawakubo's distinct unwillingness to please—and the resulting artistic purity of her clothes—Comme des Garçons appeals to both critics and a niche of adventurous consumers. And unlike most big fashion brands, it remains independent: it's not owned by a large conglomerate.

Kawakubo's success has been all her own, and she's achieved it without turning herself into a celebrity for the sake of the brand. She's known for being publicity-shy; she no longer makes appearances at her shows. She gives interviews very sparingly, and generally avoids spilling too many details about her private life. "Are there people who really wish to explain themselves?" she has asked. "You have to know me through my clothes." And people clearly feel they do: her brand has a cultlike devotion among its fans, who see clothing as a way to stand out rather than a way to blend in.

FASHION CONGLOMERATES

Many fashion brands are owned by conglomerates— big corporations that own and control many smaller companies. The two biggest fashion conglomerates are LVMH (which owns Dior, Givenchy, and Marc Jacobs, among other labels) and Kerin (which owns Gucci, Saint Laurent, Alexander McQueen, and more).

FASHION SPOTLIGHT
Björk

FULL NAME:

Björk Guðmundsdóttir

BORN:

November 21, 1965, Reykjavík, Iceland

OCCUPATION:

Musician, composer, actress

BAD GIRL CRED:

**Björk's whole life has been a lesson
in nonconformity.**

Björk may be the only person to ever wear a dress made from a stuffed animal to an awards show. Her Swan Dress was a hot topic for gossip blogs in the 2000s, and it looks exactly as it sounds: an enormous white stuffed swan (complete with eyes and beak) that wrapped around the petite, dark-haired performer's body. When she wore it to the 2001 Academy Awards, as a nominee for Best Original Song for the film *Dancer in the Dark* (which she also starred in), onlookers were shocked—even more so when she laid fake eggs beneath her white tulle skirt. For the Icelandic singer, it was a protest against the boring procession of fancy dresses at awards events, but in her world, it was hardly unusual: she's always fought against the rules of fashion.

As a child, Björk took to the spotlight early, after her performance at a school recital was sent to a local radio station by her teachers—she landed a recording contract and released her first album at age eleven. After that, she honed her anti-establishment aesthetic in a number of bands, including a teenage stint in a punk group called Spit and Snot. By 1983 she had joined anarcho-punk group Kukl, which toured with the influential English punk group Crass. Kukl appeared on live TV in 1986, with a heavily pregnant Björk wearing a belly-baring shirt that said "Like a Virgin": the ultimate ironic statement. One elderly viewer found this so offensive that she had a heart attack.

In the 1990s, after performing with pop group The Sugarcubes, Björk emerged as a solo performer, and one who took both performance and her image very seriously. On her first album, *Debut*, she flirted with different musical styles and played with strange howling, chirping vocals. She experimented with her look, too: in the music video for "Big Time Sensuality," she danced in a flatbed truck while wearing a cropped sweater and a head full of topknots that made her look like a possessed pixie, a signature look for her during this era. She maintained it through her second album, *Post*; for one of the singles from this album, "Isobel" (about a girl who rejects society to live in the wilderness), she wears a Comme des Garçons dress in a surreal video directed by Michel Gondry.

In 1997, Björk experienced a traumatic incident when an obsessed fan tried to send her a letter bomb (which was luckily intercepted). In reaction, she retreated from society and rejected her earlier, pixie-like image. For her album *Homogenic*, she had then upcoming designer Alexander McQueen design the clothes for the cover, on which she looked like an intimidating, powerful alien. And as her music became more and more experimental, her look did, too. By the mid-'00s, she'd almost entirely rejected anything that was pretty or easily understood. Her 2004 album *Medúlla* is composed of bizarre vocal performances, while her look became overtly theatrical: the album art includes strange sculptures made from her hair. In public performances, she often wore things that landed somewhere in between art and clothing; her pin-headed outfit at the Bonnaroo Music Festival in 2013 looked like something out of a horror film.

Björk's defiantly nonconformist approach to dressing has inspired others—it's easy to see her influence in the work of edgy female performers like Grimes and Fever Ray. Fashion designers have taken inspiration, too; the Italian designer Valentino made his own version of her Swan Dress for his 2014 couture show. Throughout her career, Björk has pushed the boundaries of what "fashion" means: there's nothing pretty or marketable about her choices. Instead, she uses clothing as part of her performance, and everyone loves her for it all the more.

Björk shocked everyone with her Swan Dress at the 2001 Academy Awards.

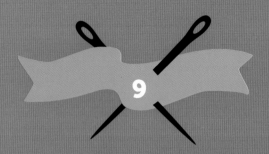

Kathleen Hanna

FASHION
Radical

FULL NAME:
Kathleen Hanna

BORN:
November 12, 1968, Portland, Oregon

OCCUPATION:
Musician, activist

BAD GIRL CRED:
Girl power wouldn't exist without Hanna,
who used her confrontational lyrics and
wardrobe to challenge a sexist culture.

It's 1992. In a dark club, a small figure stands onstage. She's wearing only a bra and skirt, and on her belly, she's scrawled a four-letter word: SLUT. She yells into the mic: "Girls to the front! I'm not kidding." And, sure enough, the guys back up and stand aside for the wave of girls who flood to the stage and gaze upward as the woman begins singing, jumping, flailing, and wailing aggressively: "Rebel girl, rebel girl, rebel girl you are the queen of my world!"

In the 1990s, girl culture desperately needed a leader, and it found one in Kathleen Hanna, front woman for the almost all-girl punk band Bikini Kill. With Bikini Kill, Hanna became famous for boldly challenging the status quo: her lyrics were confrontational, and her outfits were, too. As the charismatic leader of the riot grrrl movement, Hanna became a feminist hero.

From GIRL to GRRRL

As a child, Kathleen Hanna always knew she'd grow up to be some sort of artist. Though she was born Portland, Oregon, her family moved around to follow her father's job changes. But by the time she was fourteen, they had settled in the Pacific Northwest. Hanna was a creative kid, and participated in dance and musical theater. But one of the most influential moments of her childhood was when her stay-at-home mom took her to see feminist icon Gloria Steinem, founder of *Ms.* magazine, speak. After that, she made collages out of cutouts from *Ms.* to create posters with slogans like "Girls can do anything." Hanna was

extremely self-determined, and wanted to create an image for herself—after she read *The Valley Girl Handbook*, she even cultivated a California "Valley girl" accent because she thought it seemed like the kind of accent a rich girl would have.

In high school, Hanna was a rule-breaker. She went to punk shows, smoked pot, and drank alcohol; she also worshipped the clothing and style of the 1950s and '60s. She was often suspended from school, and was enrolled in special programs designed to help students get off drugs. She got pregnant at age fifteen but saved money from her job at McDonald's and paid for an abortion herself. "I'm really, really passionate about pro-choice, because I wouldn't be here talking to you right now if I'd had a kid at fifteen," she told *Salon* magazine in 2004.

Misbehavior notwithstanding, Hanna graduated from high school in 1986.

It's 1989 at the Evergreen State College library building, and punk music blares while cocky girls wearing silk-screened, punk-style clothes strut down the stairs. They pose, they grin, they dance to the music. One of the models, with a short blonde buzzcut, wears a dress that stands out from the rest: a long gown, it reads, ominously, "As he drug her upstairs by her neck."

This was Kathleen Hanna's fashion show, part of her photography degree at the famously creative, unconventional Evergreen State College in Washington State. For the show, Hanna had silk-screened her own artwork onto clothes she'd made herself. One night, while Hanna was in her studio working late, her roommate woke up to find a man standing over her bed. He tried to assault her, but she fought him off. When Hanna came home to her beaten-up roommate, she vowed not to let this happen again. And so her activism seeped into her work. The dress she made for the fashion show, describing her friend's attack, was her way of facing down the way she felt.

GIRL *in a Band*

Hanna also brought her fury into spoken-word performances, until she went to a workshop by Kathy Acker, a feminist experimental novelist. She told Acker that she wanted to be heard, and Acker told her, "Then why are you doing spoken word? You should be in a band." The rest was history: Bikini Kill was formed in October 1990, with Kathleen Hanna as the front woman, Kathi Wilcox on bass, Tobi Vail on drums, and Billy Karren (the lone guy) on guitar. Their 1991 demo was titled *Revolution Girl Style Now!*, a slogan meant to inspire girls to participate in a culture rooted in bands, zines, and feminism. The band performed fiery, angry, feminist punk rock, with songs like "Rebel Girl" and "Double Dare Ya" encouraging girls to embrace life with confidence and attitude.

Hanna had met Tobi Vail through a feminist fanzine called *Jigsaw*. Vail was the editor, and Hanna, an admirer of the zine, had written in to submit. So when the two began collaborating on Bikini Kill, they decided to create a zine to promote the band and its pro-girl agenda.

PUNK

Punk is an aggressive, anti-authoritarian genre of music that began in the 1970s with bands like the Sex Pistols, the Clash, and the Ramones. Punk songs were loud and fast-paced, and often political, with lyrics that challenged the status quo. Despite its rejection of the establishment, the punk scene was largely dominated by all-male bands (though there were some successful female artists, like Patti Smith and the Slits). That gender imbalance was still obvious when Bikini Kill burst onto the scene in the '90s to give punk a female face.

They called the zine *Bikini Kill*, and it featured collages and writing about the punk-rock scene, criticizing its male-dominated culture. Riot grrrl culture spread across the country and around the world, and a new generation of girls learned about feminism.

MAKING A ZINE

A zine (rhymes with "bean") is a handmade, magazine-like pamphlet that people make to share their views, stories, or photos (and, sometimes, fashion)—kind of like the paper version of a blog. Zines were often used in the punk scene because they were cheap to make and easy to distribute ... and they were a good way to spread information about topics the mainstream press wasn't interested in. Zines were a big part of promoting DIY ("do it yourself") culture. The riot grrrl movement emphasized DIY in many ways—people made their own music, made their own zines, and made or altered their own clothes.

Tying into the energy of DIY culture, fashion played a large role in the way Bikini Kill presented themselves. Hanna would buy large thrift-store T-shirts, cut them up, and refashion them as other things—headbands and skirts, for example. She also toyed around with traditional female imagery, like waitress and Girl Scout uniforms. Many of Bikini Kill's songs addressed sexism and abuse, and Hanna used her sexuality like a weapon: she dressed provocatively, in short skirts and sometimes only underwear, and wrote things like "SLUT" on her body, the idea being that reclaiming derogatory words used against women could take away some of their shaming power. While wearing these outfits, she danced, postured, and swaggered, howling lyrics like "Don't need your protection, don't need no kiss goodnight, don't need you don't need you, us girls don't need you!" Famously, at Bikini Kill shows, Hanna would call all the girls to the front so that they could enjoy the show without having to fight for space or be groped by men. Sometimes she even plunged into the crowd to remove a man who was causing trouble with girls. Despite her short stature—she was only five foot four—Hanna was an intimidating force.

Opposite: Some classic punk album covers, clockwise from top left: The Ramones, Dead Kennedys, The Sex Pistols, Savage Republic, The Clash.

NDO

**NEVER MIND
THE BOLLOCKS**

HERE'S THE

SeX PiSTOLS

SAVAGE
REPUBLIC

TRAGIC FIGURES

ICONIC LOOK № 9

SHORT PUNKY HAIR

RIPPED SHIRT

TARTAN SKIRT

VIVIENNE WESTWOOD

Rightly hailed as the Queen of Punk, VIVIENNE WESTWOOD (alongside longtime partner Malcolm McLaren) dreamed up a new aesthetic in the 1970s. Over time, her signature look changed, but in the early '70s she set the tone for what punk was. Her bleach-blonde, razored hair supposedly inspired David Bowie's haircut, while the rest of her ensemble—distressed and ripped logo tees, images of the queen with safety pins through her lip, tartan skirts—confronted a public used to more conservative dressing and gave the new punk movement an identity.

FASHION SPOTLIGHT
Beth Ditto

FULL NAME:

Mary Beth Patterson

BORN:

February 19, 1981, Judsonia, Arkansas

OCCUPATION:

Musician

BAD GIRL CRED:

**Beth Ditto's plus-size body pride
has made her a fashion icon.**

In 2009, Beth Ditto appeared naked on the cover of British fashion magazine *LOVE*. This wasn't just any undressed model: this was a fat girl, naked and glamorous, wearing heavy makeup and clutching a piece of tulle, owning the moment. It was a controversial cover that brought attention to the lack of diverse women's bodies in fashion—and heralded Ditto as the poster girl for the contemporary fat acceptance movement.

Ditto grew up poor in small-town Arkansas, but she took a different path from her classmates. She permed her hair and dyed it bright colors with Kool-Aid, and wore masculine T-shirts and jeans that got her labeled "butch." Ditto did come out as a lesbian eventually, and moved with her friends Kathy Mendonca and Nathan Howdeshell to Olympia, Washington, the epicenter of riot grrrl culture, in 1999. Soon after, the friends banded together to become the disco-punk group The Gossip (later just Gossip), and Ditto rose to fame as their full-voiced, flamboyantly dressed front woman.

The band released a few albums in the early 2000s, but it was 2007's *Standing in the Way of Control* that pushed them into the spotlight. The title song off the album was a hit, and it was political, too: the lyrics addressed then president Bush's attempts to constitutionally outlaw same-sex marriage in the United States.

That same year, Ditto began writing a column for the *Guardian* newspaper called "What would Beth Ditto do?" In it, she put her fat pride into words, saying, "Reclaiming the word fat was the most empowering step in my progress. I stopped using it for insult or degradation and instead replaced it with truth, because the truth is that I am fat, and that's ok."

Ditto, never one to blend in, refused all the rules commonly thrown at fat girls: wear slimming colors, hide your figure. Instead, she donned brightly colored dresses, figure-hugging sheaths, and horizontal stripes. The fashion world noticed. By 2008, she was a model for the designer Johnny Blue Eyes, who encouraged her to wear Lycra (Ditto approved). She started receiving top designer invites, and attended the opening of an Alexander McQueen boutique wearing a custom-made McQueen gown. By 2009, Ditto had been tapped by plus-size U.K. shop Evans to design a line. There were reports that she had already turned down a similar design deal with another major chain because, like many stores, they didn't stock clothing above a U.S. size 12 or 14. The clothes Ditto created were loud, flamboyant, and attention-catching: the sort of stuff a woman wears when she's proud of the way she looks. She posed on the cover of *LOVE* that same year, and in 2010, she walked down the catwalk in a show for Jean Paul Gaultier.

In 2013, Ditto married her girlfriend, Kristin Ogata, at a private ceremony in Hawaii, wearing a dramatic, low-cut Jean Paul Gaultier dress with a full skirt. Ever the nonconformist, she walked down the aisle barefoot. And in early 2016, Ditto made the jump to become an independent designer, releasing a self-titled fashion line with bold, fun designs in sizes 14 to 24. Her debut was warmly covered in the media. "Instead of the idea of being 'flattering,'" as she told *Vogue*, her fashions were "just really interesting and cool."

Though she's just one woman, Ditto's influence has been profound: her wild style and clothing-biz success have proven that fashion is for everyone—no matter what size they wear.

Beth Ditto aims to stand out, not blend in, with her fashion choices. She's pictured here at the Cannes Film Festival in 2010.

ASKING *for it*

As more and more people flocked to see Bikini Kill, Hanna was subjected to a lot of criticism. Not all men appreciated her aggressively pro-female stance, and sometimes they threatened her and the band. But it wasn't just men: as she told *New York* magazine in 2013, "Women were saying we weren't doing feminism right, journalists were like, 'somebody should put tape on her mouth.'" And so, at the 1993 abortion rights show Rock for Choice, Hanna wore a snug, red sleeveless dress emblazoned with the words "KILL ME"—a message designed to ask her critics what, exactly, constituted "asking for it." Hanna made the dress herself, and ironed on the letters.

In 1997, Hanna took a break from Bikini Kill and produced, in her bedroom, a solo album, which she released under the name Julie Ruin. When she decided to put together a live band for the project, she began to work with her friends Sadie Benning and Johanna Fateman—and their work together ultimately became the band Le Tigre.

Le Tigre was, simply, a feminist party band. They played up-tempo, fun electroclash songs that people could dance to—but those songs happened to have socially conscious, feminist lyrics. The band often wore color-coordinated, matching outfits, and their music was celebratory—which opened up their messages to a wider audience. One of the more memorable matchy-matchy ensembles the band donned was printed with an all-over pattern reading "Stop Bush," in reference to U.S. president George W. Bush, whose pro-war stance and right-wing politics were unpopular with feminists.

Though Le Tigre was successful, Hanna left the band in 2005, claiming she'd already said everything she needed to say. But then, in 2013, a documentary film about her life, *The Punk Singer*, was released. Though she was only in her forties, it was the sort of thing that's usually made when a performer is near the end of her days. In it, Hanna made a surprising revelation: the real reason she had quit was because she was sick. She had been diagnosed with Lyme disease, an illness caused by a tick bite that can cause a debilitating mix of symptoms.

Opposite: Le Tigre members JD Samson (who replaced Benning in 2000), Fateman, and Hanna with a koala in Australia. Above: Hanna playing the drums.

It turned out that Hanna agreed to make *The Punk Singer* because she thought she might die, and she wanted one last chance to be heard. Despite her worries, she managed to keep going, and formed a new band called The Julie Ruin, named after her '90s solo project. She still plays with fashion, too. When the 2013 book *The Riot Grrrl Collection* came out, documenting the '90s riot grrrl era, Hanna, alongside longtime collaborator Kathi Wilcox, launched a fashion collection for a fashion-themed social networking site.

One of the items was a "KILL ME" dress, a replica of her controversial 1993 Rock for Choice outfit.

Hanna's personal riot grrrl tendencies clearly haven't dissipated, and her early days with Bikini Kill continue to influence feminist rebellion. From the performance art protests of Russian punk band Pussy Riot to the anti-rape, flaunt-your-sexuality Slut Walk protests, Hanna's touch is everywhere. If there ever was a Revolution Girl Style, it's definitely happening now.

Pussy Riot in 2012, channeling riot grrrl energy in their protest tactics.

FASHION SPOTLIGHT
Pussy Riot

MOST PROMINENT MEMBERS:
**Nadya Tolokonnikova, Masha Alyokhina,
and Yekaterina Samutsevich**

FORMED:
August 2011, Moscow, Russia

PURPOSE:
Political protest through punk rock

BAD GIRL CRED:
**Their brash, radical protests have made
Pussy Riot enemies of the Russian state.**

On February 21, 2012, everything was quiet in Moscow's Cathedral of Christ the Savior. Orthodox Christian women wearing headscarves prayed, and a handful of tourists walked around, snapping photos of the ornate, golden inside of the church.

And then, in a flurry of color, five girls wearing a brightly hued mishmash of balaclavas, short dresses, and color-blocked tights leaped onto the pulpit, instruments raised, and burst into a cacophony of song. "Banish Putin, banish Putin!" they screamed as security guards tried to drag them from the stage. The women were members of the protest group Pussy Riot, and their recording of this performance, entitled "Punk Prayer— Mother of God, Chase Putin Away!" was a music video by later that day. (You can still find it on YouTube.)

Pussy Riot is a Russian feminist activist collective who use music, art, and fashion to stage their protests. Founded in 2011, they rose to fame after their "Punk Prayer" performance at the cathedral in Moscow, where they so memorably opposed the autocratic rule of Russian president Vladimir Putin (known for things like imprisoning journalists and opponents, controlling the media, and appointing his friends to powerful positions). Three of the group—Nadya Tolokonnikova, Masha Alyokhina, and Yekaterina Samutsevich— were arrested soon after the protest on charges of hooliganism, and went through what many people thought was a show trial (a court case staged to scare the public and make a political point). They were all jailed in 2012. What was Vladimir Putin trying to say? Why, that dissidents wouldn't be tolerated! But Pussy Riot weren't afraid, and their image spread across news reports and social media around the world. Numerous Western celebrities publicly announced their support of the group (Madonna, Björk, and Patti Smith are just a few), and, at some protests, people dressed up as Pussy Riot in solidarity. By 2014, all three of the women were out of jail; Tolokonnikova and Alyokhina, the two most famous of the group, went on to form a separate prison reform organization called Zona Prava.

Pussy Riot's signature look—face-concealing balaclava, short dress, and brightly colored tights, all color-blocked and contrasting—was and is a key aspect of their protest tactics. In a feature in *T Magazine*, Petya Verzilov, Tolokonnikova's husband, summed up their approach nicely: "The way they present their performances is a bright, feminist splash in our gray Russian politics and society."

Pussy Riot's look does more than just confront the conservatism of their home country. It's also extremely easy to mimic: all any girl needs is a beanie, some scissors to cut eyeholes, a dress, and some tights. Dressing this way, any girl immediately aligns herself with Pussy Riot's punk protest—and many did so in marches in the U.S. and other countries demanding the girls' freedom.

An activist in Moscow picketing for Pussy Riot to be freed from jail in 2013.

10

Lady Gaga

FASHION

Freak

FULL NAME:
Stefani Joanne Angelina Germanotta

BORN:
March 28, 1986, Manhattan, New York

OCCUPATION:
Musician

BAD GIRL CRED:
If it's bizarre, shocking, or totally ridiculous, Lady Gaga has probably worn it. In doing so, she's flown the freak flag for anyone who feels a little different.

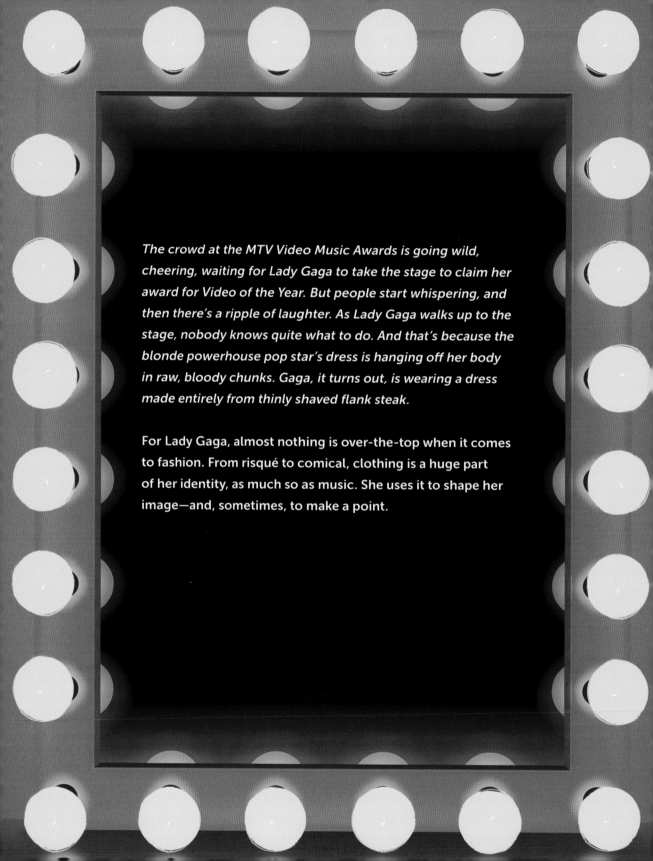

The crowd at the MTV Video Music Awards is going wild, cheering, waiting for Lady Gaga to take the stage to claim her award for Video of the Year. But people start whispering, and then there's a ripple of laughter. As Lady Gaga walks up to the stage, nobody knows quite what to do. And that's because the blonde powerhouse pop star's dress is hanging off her body in raw, bloody chunks. Gaga, it turns out, is wearing a dress made entirely from thinly shaved flank steak.

For Lady Gaga, almost nothing is over-the-top when it comes to fashion. From risqué to comical, clothing is a huge part of her identity, as much so as music. She uses it to shape her image—and, sometimes, to make a point.

BORN
This Way

She may be a chart-topping musician whose ultra-passionate followers adore her for her freakish, fashion-forward style and outspoken support of LGBT rights and anti-bullying campaigns, but Lady Gaga wasn't born famous. In fact, when she came into the world in 1986, she was a totally normal kid named Stefani Germanotta. She grew up on Manhattan's Upper West Side, and her parents sent her to an exclusive Catholic school called Sacred Heart. She was a spirited theater girl, known for creating elaborate costumes for stage productions. She was also a big fan of music, and participated in open-mic nights with a classic rock cover band that she started.

Gaga followed high school with a short-lived experiment with higher education. She dropped out after her second year at the Tisch School of the Arts at New York University, in 2005, to pursue another goal: to become a rock star. Her family put up with it on the condition that she'd go back to school if it didn't work out. She formed another group, called the Stefani Germanotta Band, dyed her hair black, and started straightening it. Her shows around New York drew only a handful of followers, until one day she was spotted by a producer, Rob Fusari, who thought she was talented. The two started working together, and dating, too. When she would walk into the studio, he would sing a song by the British rock band Queen, "Radio Ga Ga," claiming it was her "entrance song." One day when Fusari was texting her, his phone's autocorrect changed "Radio" to "Lady"; when she got the text that said "Lady Gaga," Germanotta knew she had found her stage name.

Around the same time, Gaga began experimenting with style. She wanted to distance herself from her Catholic schoolgirl past, so her ensembles were provocative. She wore shorter and shorter skirts until she stopped wearing skirts altogether: underwear became her outerwear. It's a look she maintained into stardom, although with her unconventional attitude and looks, the effect was often as strange as it was sexy. Soon after, she signed a deal with a record label but was quickly dropped. Devastated, she devoted herself more intensely to music. She found a new collaborator, a cabaret entertainer named Lady Starlight. The two performed together: Gaga would throw on a bikini, fingerless black gloves, and Lucite heels, and go-go dance as part of the act. She was firmly on the path to being a fashion freak.

Another label-signing happened soon after, but Gaga had some concerns. She thought that with her large nose and eccentric Italian beauty, she didn't resemble a traditional pop princess. But rather than cave to pressure, she found inspiration in the artist Andy Warhol: an unusual-looking man, in the 1960s he turned his eccentricity into a vehicle to promote his art. Warhol was also intensely interested in his own appearance and underwent many transformations throughout his life, dressing flamboyantly as part of his identity.

And so Gaga had found her muse. Soon after this revelatory moment, in 2008, she moved to L.A. to form the Haus of Gaga, a creative team inspired

ANDY WARHOL + THE FACTORY

The Factory was pop artist Andy Warhol's New York studio from the 1960s through the mid-'80s. It was also a hip hotspot where artists and groupies would hang out, hoping to soak up some of Warhol's creative energy and fame. At the Factory, Andy would groom "superstars," muses he would paint and put into his films. These Factory superstars often had a certain look: edgy and avant-garde. Many of them were also drag queens.

by Andy Warhol's Factory. From clothing to makeup and props, the Haus of Gaga was responsible for building a daring, avant-garde look for Gaga. Based on her obsession with Andy Warhol, Gaga also became fascinated by androgyny, and began styling herself after Liza Minnelli, a cabaret star who is also a gay icon.

Andy Warhol, pop art legend, immortalized in wax at Madame Tussauds.

ICONIC LOOK № 10

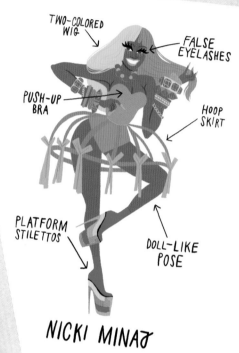

TWO-COLORED WIG

FALSE EYELASHES

PUSH-UP BRA

HOOP SKIRT

PLATFORM STILETTOS

DOLL-LIKE POSE

NICKI MINAJ

The rapper **NICKI MINAJ** is a master of disguises. As part of her performance, she assumes the role of "alter egos" who allow her to explore different modes of self-expression. The most famous is Harajuku Barbie, as whom Minaj wears ultra-girly clothes and a lot of pink. Another of her alter egos, Roman Zolanski (who she's now retired), was a blonde gay male who wore all black. Outside of performance, Minaj's outfits are even wilder: she creatively mixes bright colors, crazy wigs, dresses covered in neon puffballs, and interesting elements like rain boots and surgical masks. With her fame as both a rapper and a style queen, designers clamor to dress her.

FASHION SPOTLIGHT
Cher

FULL NAME:

Cherilyn Bono (née Sarkisian)

BORN:

May 20, 1946, El Centro, California

OCCUPATION:

Singer, actress, model

BAD GIRL CRED:

**Cher's flamboyance has inspired a
generation of fashionable freaks.**

"I feel like a bumper car," Cher told *Vanity Fair* magazine in 2010. "If I hit a wall, I'm backing up and going in another direction." And that's true: the half-Armenian, part-white, part-Cherokee singer and film star has had a wild career that has gone in many directions, but constant throughout it all has been her ability to grab the public's eye through her spirited performances marked by showstopping fashion choices.

Young Cher, who always dreamed of being famous, dropped out of school and moved out of her mom's house at sixteen. She danced in Los Angeles clubs and tirelessly networked in the hopes of making her dreams of fame come true, and soon met a performer named Sonny Bono, a man eleven years older than her. Married in 1964 when Cher was only eighteen, the two had a rocky relationship. But as a singer–songwriter duo, the couple fared better: their number-one hit "I Got You Babe" landed Cher in the public eye. Soon people were imitating her (and Sonny's) hippie aesthetic, which included bell-bottom pants, ruffled shirts, and vests. But Cher's style didn't truly take off until she and Sonny wound up on TV in the '70s with a show called *The Sonny & Cher Comedy Hour*.

And that style, it turned out, was outrageous. For the run of the show, Cher enlisted the talents of a designer named Bob Mackie, who dressed her in costumes that were sometimes extremely wild. One that she wore in 1973, which involved a feathered headdress and an exposed navel, caused her to receive a reprimand from the television network, CBS—in those days, bellybuttons were rarely seen on TV.

Sonny and Cher soon divorced, and Cher moved on. In the years that followed, she bounced between music and movies. As it turns out, she was an excellent actress, and her role in the film *Silkwood* earned her an Oscar nomination. But when she was snubbed by the Oscars for her following film, *Mask*, in 1986, she showed them what she thought of their snooty opinions ("They said I didn't dress like a serious actress and my boyfriends were too young," she quipped) by wearing the wildest, most provocative dress ever seen at the awards show. Made by Bob Mackie, it featured an enormous black headdress, a spangled bra-top, a bare midriff, a floor-length beaded skirt, and a black cape. But the Academy forgave her, and in 1990, she won an Oscar for her role in *Moonstruck*—which she accepted wearing a see-through beaded gown paired with a dramatic black wrap.

It was a far different world from

when she'd been on TV in the '70s;
by 1990, people were used to seeing
Cher nearly naked all over their TVs,
clad almost solely in huge wigs and
spangles. In fact, just the year before,
her music video for the song "If I Could
Turn Back Time" was famously banned
from MTV; in it, Cher danced on a
U.S. battleship for a group of cheering
sailors while wearing only a body
stocking and a revealing bathing suit.
The Navy was not amused.

In the years that followed, Cher's
public presence was unflagging. She
staged a "comeback" in the late '90s,
transforming herself into an electronic-
music diva—and cementing her role as
a gay icon. The gay community loved
her drama, glamour, and rags-to-riches
rise to fame (and, later, her child Chaz
Bono's coming-out as a lesbian, and
eventually as a trans man). In 2014, Cher
was still touring with new music, her
stage costumes reliably over-the-top as
always, and usually including enormous
headdresses. By then, Cher's cultural
importance was firmly established, and
a new generation of pop starlets were
walking in her glitter-strewn footsteps.
Some openly copied her, but Cher
didn't mind. In 2014, Lady Gaga
actually borrowed her idol's 1980s
wigs, turning back time in a nod
to Cher's enormous influence.

Cher at the 2010 VMAs, wearing the ensemble
that got her video for "If I Could Turn Back Time"
banned from MTV in 1989.

IT'S ALL FOR *Show*

Gaga, showing off, as usual.

By 2009, Lady Gaga's first album had made her a legitimate star: songs like "Just Dance" and "Poker Face" were huge successes, and the videos that accompanied them, complete with over-the-top costuming and plotlines, were infamous. They often explored themes of sex, violence, and power, hardly the sort of mainstream-friendly subjects you would expect from a Top 40 artist. Like her hero, Andy Warhol, Gaga turned her whole life into a performance, and was never seen out of costume. Even when she was dressed up in the most stereotypically female outfits—dresses, heels, and makeup—her femininity took on aspects of performance. Whenever she was out in public, she was always wearing something as daring and outré as her music-video ensembles, to the point where most people didn't even know what she really looked like.

In late 2009, Gaga released a new EP, *The Fame Monster*, which contained the single "Bad Romance." The video for the song involved futuristic alien and monster motifs and a lot of white PVC (stretchy plastic fabric). Throughout the video, Gaga and her dancers raise their fists in symbolic monster claws; the gesture was adopted by Gaga's fan base, who called themselves the Little Monsters, as a greeting. The Little Monsters—numbering among them many gay, bisexual, and transgender teens—rallied around the idea of Gaga as their "Mother Monster," a sort of patron saint for people who considered themselves outsiders or freaks. (In 2011, she started a social networking site for them, called littlemonsters.com.) Little Monsters prided themselves on their flamboyant, often homemade outfits and accessories, crazy makeup and hair, and embrace of art and fashion.

That same year, Gaga appeared on the MTV Video Music Awards in her infamous Meat Dress—intended to protest the U.S. military's "don't ask, don't tell" policy, which prevented openly gay and lesbian citizens from serving. Animal-rights groups condemned the outfit, and few people understood the political point Gaga was trying to make (as she explained to talk-show host Ellen DeGeneres on TV later that night,

"If we don't stand up for what we believe in and if we don't fight for our rights, pretty soon we're going to have as much rights as the meat on our own bones.") But at the very least, Gaga had proven that she knew how to get attention.

Gaga in 2009, raising her hand in a "monster claw" greeting to her fans.

LADY GAGA'S CRAZIEST OUTFITS

The Pink Burqa: (opposite page, bottom) Gaga walked the catwalk at milliner (hat designer) Philip Treacy's 2013 show wearing a translucent pink cape dress that resembled a burqa, to much controversy.

The Meat Dress: (opposite page, right) In 2010, Lady Gaga appeared on the MTV VMAs in a dress, hat, and shoes made from raw steak. Even the clutch (handbag) she carried was meat.

Lobster Claw Shoes: (opposite page, left) In her video for "Bad Romance" (2009), Gaga wore some truly alien-looking heels, designed by Alexander McQueen, that resembled lobster claws.

The Kermit Sweater: In 2009, Lady Gaga appeared on German TV wearing a sweater made entirely from Kermit the Frog stuffed animals.

The See-Through Habit: In 2011, Gaga performed in Florida in a see-through Latex nun's habit, with electrician's tape concealing her nipples.

The Fly Eyes: (opposite page, top left) For a live TV performance in 2010, Gaga wore huge bejeweled goggles.

HEY BOY *Hey Girl*

On the cover of Vogue Hommes Japan, *a dark-haired young man poses, sultry and masculine in black and white. The tagline says "Jo Calderone, too cool to care." Inside the magazine there is a short interview with the mystery man, who claims to be a mechanic who knows Lady Gaga. When asked to explain his relationship to the pop star, he says: "I met her at a shoot Nick Knight was doing … She's fuckin' beautiful, and funny, and interesting. I was a little nervous for Nick to start shooting. She said, 'Don't be baby, you were born this way.' I took her out after. The rest is private."*

Around the time of Gaga's first album, a rumor began to circulate: that she was, in fact, intersex, meaning she had both male and female parts. Though gay rights had come a long way by 2009, there was still little mainstream discussion of concepts like intersexuality, transgenderism, or gender identity. The suggestion that a female pop star wasn't fully "female" could have destroyed her career. Lady Gaga, however, brushed off the rumor, and, though she later denied it in a TV interview, made it clear she wasn't bothered. "I portray myself in a very androgynous way, and I love androgyny," she said.

Gaga's toying with gender reached its peak with Jo Calderone—her male alter ego. After debuting him in a fashion editorial in *Vogue Hommes*, Gaga took him further: he appeared in the music video for "You and I," and performed on the 2011 MTV VMAs. Notably, she stayed in character all night. Some viewers were confused

In late 2012, Gaga picked another cause to champion: the body. At the time, she was the subject of a round of cruel tabloid photographs that showed that her once-lithe figure had filled out somewhat, and speculation built about her weight gain. In response, Gaga posted a photo of herself, wearing only her underwear, on her social networking site, with the caption "Bulimia and anorexia since I was 15." She created a subsection on her littlemonsters.com site called Body Revolution, calling for bravery and compassion. "Be brave and celebrate with us your 'perceived flaws' as society tells us. May we make our flaws famous, and thus redefine the heinous," she told her fans, and they began posting photos of themselves. It was another example of Gaga twisting a supposed flaw to her advantage, and using it to empower her fans.

Gaga's devotion to staying in character, dressed to the nines, is astounding. Whether she's playing an alien creature or a piece of meat, a swarthy man or an ultrafeminine diva, she makes the point that all clothing is, in a sense, a costume—a way to explore different identities. As a famous performer willing to share her weaknesses with her fans, in the hopes of inspiring them to greater self-acceptance, Gaga uses her flamboyance in both clothing and behavior to make a powerful point: it's a great thing to be unusual.

about the performance, and some considered it a publicity stunt; others thought of it as a statement from Gaga about the fluidity of gender. The arrival of Jo coincided with Gaga's release of her third album, *Born This Way*. The title song off the album was a call to arms for equality, regardless of race, sexual orientation, or religious affiliation, and it became an anthem for the gay pride movement. Inspired by this, she started the Born This Way Foundation, a charity aimed at "empowering [young people] to create a kinder and braver world"; some of its initiatives included anti-bullying and anti-homophobia campaigns.

FASHION SPOTLIGHT
Isabella Blow

FULL NAME:
Isabella Delves Blow (née Broughton)

BORN:
November 19, 1958, London, England

OCCUPATION:
Fashion director

BAD GIRL CRED:
Blow's eccentric wardrobe is the stuff of legend.

Daphne Guinness

FULL NAME:

Daphne Diana Joan Susanna Guinness

BORN:

November 9, 1967, London, England

OCCUPATION:

Socialite, style icon

BAD GIRL CRED:

Her wild style has made Guinness a fashion muse.

Believe it or not, this is a hat. Philip Treacy's designs were wild, which is why they were so beloved by Blow.

In 2010, the fashion world was aflutter when eccentric British style icon Isabella Blow's wardrobe went on the block at Christie's auction house. Blow's wild fashion sense was the stuff of legend. A fashion-magazine editor, she had a sharp eye for emerging talent, and she spotted and nurtured soon-to-be massive designers like Philip Treacy and Alexander McQueen. She was famous for her bizarre and wonderful Treacy hats; she was quoted as saying, "Fashion is a vampiric thing, it's the hoover on your brain. That's why I wear the hats, to keep everyone away from me." Tragically, though, Blow suffered from depression, and committed suicide in 2007 at age forty-eight. Seeing Blow's wardrobe up for sale struck a nerve with her grieving friend, heiress and style icon Daphne Guinness—who made headlines when she scooped up Blow's entire wardrobe in one lot.

If there was anybody who would give Blow's clothing collection the respect it deserved, it was Guinness. The two first met at a party, and assisted each other on fashion shoots, sparking a lifelong friendship. Guinness was another notable fashion eccentric: she too was friends with Alexander McQueen, and she was known for wearing strange and unusual ensembles: shoes with no heels, all-silver catsuits, futuristic kimonos.

When she couldn't find an item she was looking for, she made it herself. A profile in *The New Yorker* described her style as that of a "slightly deranged fairy."

Both Blow and Guinness paved the way for a certain kind of fashion: wild and experimental, artistic and extroverted. It's easy to see their style reflected in that of people like Nicki Minaj and Lady Gaga; in fact, Gaga has acknowledged their influence on her look, saying, "Isabella and Daphne are two exceptional human beings, women, icons. And more than that! They have helped me look inside myself. I've examined their lives and their personalities in order to understand myself better. Daphne, like Isabella, is a huge source of inspiration for me. I cherish their lives. I cherish them both. It is as if we are all cut from the same cloth."

After Blow's death, Guinness set up the Isabella Blow Foundation, with the dual goal of encouraging emerging fashion designers (much like Blow did) and increasing awareness of mental illness. And in tribute to her friend, Guinness collected the clothes she purchased at auction and turned them into a museum exhibit, which went on display in 2013. The collection captures the unbridled creativity with which Blow approached dressing, and life.

Daphne Guinness at a charity fashion show in 2010, walking the runway in an otherworldly Alexander McQueen ensemble.

Conclusion

Following the complex life stories of the women in this book, it's obvious that fashion is about more than just clothes—it's been a powerful tool for communication for a long, long time. Cleopatra and Marie Antoinette, queens from eras hundreds of years apart, used fashion to prove their worth as leaders to all who watched them. Coco Chanel and Rei Kawakubo, designers who dressed two different generations, used it to redefine feminine beauty. For Frida Kahlo, an artist from the early twentieth century, fashion was deeply symbolic, and she worked it into both her art and her life in a way that captured the public imagination. Lady Gaga and Madonna, both entertainers, pushed the boundaries of what's acceptable for a woman to wear (for totally different reasons, in different decades). Marlene Dietrich, a star from the early days of film, used her wardrobe to toy with gender roles, while Kathleen Hanna, a '90s musician, used hers to protest them. And Diana Vreeland, a magazine editor from the '60s, had such a peculiar and inspiring way of looking at clothes that it has shaped the way we consume fashion to this day.

But while all of these women used clothes to serve their purposes, none of them let themselves be defined wholly by what they wore. What they all have in common is an unshakeable will to live life on their own terms. By breaking the rules, these bad girls changed what's expected of women in fashion— and in life.

SELECTED REFERENCES

Chapter 1
Chang, Jung. (2013). *Empress Dowager Cixi: The Concubine Who Launched Modern China*. New York: Knopf.

Fletcher, Joann. (2008). *Cleopatra the Great: The Woman behind the Legend*. London: Hodder & Stoughton.

Miles, Margaret M., ed. (2011). *Cleopatra: A Sphinx Revisited*. Berkeley: University of California Press.

Rothman, Lily. (2014). "There's a Very Good Reason Why Katy Perry's 'Dark Horse' Video Is Set in Ancient Egypt," *Time*, August 28. At time.com/9233/katy-perry-dark-horse-egypt/.

Marks, Ben. (2013). "Trailing Angela Davis, from FBI Flyers to 'Radical Chic' Art." *Collectors Weekly*, July 3. At www.collectorsweekly.com/articles/angela-davis-from-fbi-flyers-to-radical-chic-art/.

Schiff, Stacy. (2010). *Cleopatra: A Life*. New York: Little, Brown.

"Symbols and Emblems Used in Elizabeth Portraiture." (n.d.). Royal Museums Greenwich. At www.rmg.co.uk/explore/sea-and-ships/in-depth/elizabeth/representing-the-queen/symbols-and-emblems-used-in-elizabeth-portraiture (accessed August 29, 2014).

Tyldesley, Joyce. (2008). *Cleopatra: Last Queen of Egypt*. New York: Basic Books.

Watkins, Susan. (2007). *Elizabeth I and Her World*. London: Thames & Hudson.

Chapter 2
"Imelda Marcos." (n.d.). Biography.com. At www.biography.com/people/imelda-marcos-21062601 (accessed October 7, 2014).

Schillinger, Liesl. (2102). "Marrying Up" [review of Anne Sebba, *That Woman*]. *New York Times*, March 9. At www.nytimes.com/2012/03/11/books/review/that-woman-by-anne-sebba.html.

Sebba, Anne, and Imogen Fox. (2011). "Wallis Simpson Used Fashion as a Weapon." *The Guardian*, September 2. At www.theguardian.com/fashion/2011/sep/02/wallis-simpson-fashion.

Weber, Caroline. (2007). *Queen of Fashion: What Marie Antoinette Wore to the Revolution*. London: Aurum.

Chapter 3
"Amelia Bloomer." (n.d.). Biography.com. At www.biography.com/people/amelia-bloomer-9216245 (accessed October 25, 2014).

"Josephine Baker." (n.d.). Biography.com. At www.biography.com/people/josephine-baker-9195959 (accessed June 15, 2015).

Paris, Barry. (1989, rpt. 2000). *Louise Brooks: A Biography*. Minneapolis: University of Minnesota Press.

Picardie, Justine. (2011). *Chanel: Her Life*. Göttingen: Steidl.

Chapter 4
Herrera, Hayden. (1983). *Frida: A Biography of Frida Kahlo*. New York: Harper Perennial.

Paracchini, Gian. (2010). *The Prada Life: A Biography*. Milan: Baldini Castoldi Dalai Editore.

Secrest, Meryle. (2014). *Elsa Schiaparelli: A Biography*. New York: Knopf.

"That's What You Call a Radical Style Change: Controversial Rapper M.I.A. Rocks a Burqa on the Red Carpet." (2010). *The Daily Mail*, October 18. At www.dailymail.co.uk/tvshowbiz/article-1321425/2010-Spike-TV-Scream-Awards-M-I-A-rocks-burqa-red-carpet.html.

Chapter 5

Harlan, Elizabeth. (2004). *George Sand*. New Haven, CT: Yale University Press.

Jack, Belinda. (2000). *George Sand: A Woman's Life Writ Large*. New York: Knopf.

Riva, Maria. (1992). *Marlene Dietrich*. New York: Ballantine Books.

Rodriguez, Leah. (2014). "Praise Diane Keaton's Glorious Menswear Style." *New York*, December 24. At nymag.com/thecut/2014/11/praise-diane-keatons-glorious-menswear-style.html.

"Twiggy." (n.d.). Biography.com. At www.biography.com/people/twiggy-9512626 (accessed December 27, 2014).

Chapter 6

"Anna Wintour." (n.d.). Biography.com. At www.biography.com/people/anna-wintour-214147 (accessed January 30, 2015).

Coddington, Grace, with Michael Roberts. (2012). *Grace: A Memoir*. New York: Random House.

Collins, Amy Fine. (1993). "The Cult of Diana." *Vanity Fair*, November. At www.vanityfair.com/culture/features/1993/11/diana-vreeland-199311.

Cutler, R. J., dir. (2009). *The September Issue*. [videocassette].

Vreeland, Lisa. (2011). *Diana Vreeland: The Eye Has to Travel*. New York: Abrams.

Witt, Emily. (2014). "Tavi Forever." *T: The New York Times Style Magazine*, June 6. At www.nytimes.com/2014/06/06/t-magazine/tavi-gevinson-on-rookie-magazine-and-growing-up.html.

Chapter 7

Crosbie, Lynn. (2012). "The Monroe Doctrine: 50 Years Later, Marilyn's Fashion Influence Endures." *Globe and Mail*, August 11. At www.theglobeandmail.com/life/fashion-and-beauty/fashion/the-monroe-doctrine-50-years-later-marilyns-fashion-influence-endures/article4471081/.

Easlea, Daryl, and Eddi Fiegel. (2012). *Madonna, Blond Ambition*. Milwaukee: Backbeat Books.

"Madonna: Biography." (n.d.). *Rolling Stone*. At www.rollingstone.com/music/artists/madonna/biography (accessed February 15, 2015).

Steinem, Gloria. (1986; rpt. 2006). "The Woman Who Will Not Die." *American Masters*. At www.pbs.org/wnet/americanmasters/episodes/marilyn-monroe/still-life/61/.

Sykes, Plum. (2014). "The Rihanna Effect: Fashion's Most Exciting Muse, On Her Third Vogue Cover." *Vogue*, February 18. At www.vogue.com/865163/rihanna-fashions-most-exciting-new-muse.

Chapter 8

"Cindy Sherman." (n.d.). Guggenheim Collection Online. At www.guggenheim.org/new-york/collections/collection-online/artists/bios/688 (accessed December 30, 2014).

Fukai, Akiko, Barbara Vinken, Susannah Frankel, and Hirofumi Kurino. (2010). *Future Beauty: 30 Years of Japanese Fashion*. London: Merrell.

Glasscock, Jessica. (n.d.). "Bridging the Art/Commerce Divide: Cindy Sherman and Rei Kawakubo of Comme des Garçons." At www.nyu.edu/greyart/exhibits/odysseys/Commerce/body_commerce.html (accessed December 30, 2014).

Horyn, Cathy. (2012). "Like Mona Lisa, Ever So Veiled." *New York Times*, May 30. At www.nytimes.com/2012/05/31/fashion/rei-kawakubo-of-comme-des-garcons-veiled-like-mona-lisa.html.

"John Lennon & Yoko Ono: Bagism Press Conference." (1969). Beatles Interview Database. At www.beatlesinterviews.org/db1969.0331.beatles.html.

Thurman, Judith. (2005). "The Misfit." *The New Yorker*, July 4. http://www.newyorker.com/
magazine/2005/07/04/the-misfit-3.

Witt, Emily. (2015). "The Peculiar Genius of Björk." *T: The New York Times Style Magazine*, January 23. At
www.nytimes.com/2015/01/23/t-magazine/the-peculiar-genius-of-bjork-vulnicura-moma.html.

Chapter 9

Anderson, Sini, dir. (2013). *The Punk Singer: A Film about Kathleen Hanna*. Prod. Sini Anderson et al.

Anderson-Minshall, Diane. (2012). "Beth Ditto Interview: Diamonds Are Forever." *The Advocate*,
December 3. At www.advocate.com/print-issue/cover-stories/2012/12/03/cover-story-interview-
gossip-front-woman-beth-ditto.

Goldman, Vivien. (2012). "The Riot Girls' Style." *T: The New York Times Style Magazine*, August 8. At
tmagazine.blogs.nytimes.com/2012/08/08/the-riot-girls-style/.

Lerner, Mike, and Maxim Pozdorovkin, dir. (2013). *Pussy Riot: A Punk Prayer*. Roast Beef Productions.

Rubin, Julia. (2013). "Kathleen Hanna on '90s Nostalgia and Teen Feminism." *Teen Vogue*, June. At
www.teenvogue.com/fashion/2013-06/bikini-kill-vfiles-kathleen-hanna/?slide=1.

Westwood, Vivienne, and Ian Kelly. (2014). *Vivienne Westwood*. London: Pan Macmillan/Picador.

Chapter 10

Alexander, Ella. (2010). "Guinness' Tribute." Vogue News, July 5. At www.vogue.co.uk/news/2010/07/05/
daphne-guinness-buys-blows-wardrobe.

Fury, Alexander. (2014). "Socialite? Muse? Actress? Punk? Daphne Guinness Continues to Defy
Expectations." *The Independent*, September 20. At www.independent.co.uk/life-style/
fashion/features/socialite-muse-actress-punk-daphne-guinness-continues-to-defy-
expectations-9738729.html.

"A Guide to the Many Personalities of Nicki Minaj." (2012). *Paper*, April 3. Online only at www.papermag.
com/2012/04/a_guide_to_the_many_personalities_of_nicki_minaj.php.

Phoenix, Helia. (2010). *Lady Gaga: Just Dance: The Biography*. London: Orion Publishing.

Sowray, Bibby. (2011). "Who's Who: Isabella Blow." *Vogue*, November 4. At www.vogue.co.uk/spy/
biographies/isabella-blow-biography.

Staples, Brent. (2012). "Nicki Minaj Crashes Hip-Hop's Boys Club." *New York Times*, July 7. At www.
nytimes.com/2012/07/08/opinion/sunday/nicki-minaj-crashes-hip-hops-boys-club.html.

FURTHER READING

Croll, Jennifer. (2014). *Fashion That Changed the World*. Munich: Prestel.

Heti, Sheila, Heidi Julavits, and Leanne Shapton. (2014). *Women in Clothes*. New York: Blue Rider Press.

Scott, Linda. (2006). *Fresh Lipstick: Redressing Fashion and Feminism*. New York: Palgrave Macmillan.

Schatz, Kate, and Miriam Klein Stahl. (2015). *Rad American Women A–Z: Rebels, Trailblazers, and
Visionaries Who Shaped Our History … and Our Future!* San Francisco: City Lights Books.

ACKNOWLEDGMENTS

My biggest, baddest thank-you goes to bad girls of publishing Paula Ayer and Colleen MacMillan at Annick for making this book a reality. Especially Paula: without her brilliant ideas and the conversations we had about being teenaged girls (we were so different in such great, contrasting ways), this book wouldn't be half as good. And to everyone else at Annick who aided and abetted this project: I'm truly grateful for your support.

Thank you as well to Stephanie Fysh (with special input from her teen daughter, Esme!) for a gentle but thoughtful copyedit, to Linda Pruessen for proofreading, and to Natalie Olsen for such a kickass design.

Last but not least, I should tip my proverbial hat to my parents for allowing me to dress like a complete weirdo—I mean, explore my identity through clothing—throughout my teenaged years. I'm better for it.

IMAGE CREDITS

INDEX

ABOUT THE AUTHOR AND ILLUSTRATOR

Jennifer Croll's first fashion statement as a frog-catching, street-hockey-playing tomboy was pairing gingham dresses with pants with ripped knees. By high school, her look had evolved to include a lot of black, and her interests included going to punk shows and writing bad poetry. Today, she's still fond of black, but has thankfully given up poetry in favor of prose.

Jennifer spent several years working in magazines, writing and editing on culture and style for publications including *NYLON*, *Adbusters*, and *Dazed and Confused*. In 2014, she published her first book, *Fashion That Changed the World*, about the cultural influences on fashion through history.

Jennifer lives in Vancouver, British Columbia, with a sharply dressed tuxedo cat.

Ada Buchholc lives in Poland and has illustrated for a wide range of clients in advertising, music, and fashion, among other industries. Her work has appeared in the *New Republic*, *Little White Lies*, and *enRoute* magazines. Ada's inspirations include the 1920s and 1990s, Ed Wood movies, *Monkey Island* games, the animated series *Samurai Jack*, and never-ending weltschmerz. She also prefers to wear black, which sometimes frightens strangers.